Pranav Pandya is an accomplished IT professional with a remarkable career spanning four decades. With enriching experiences in India, the Middle East, the USA and Europe, he has established himself as a business development expert with a deep understanding of global markets. In recent years, he has embarked on a conscious journey to prioritise his other passions: photography, travelling, music, and writing. Born and raised in Mumbai, he draws inspiration from the city's vibrant culture, rich history and can-do attitude.

Mindful Productivity
by Pranav Pandya
Paperback Edition

First Published in 2023 in India by

Inkfeathers Publishing
Vivek Vihar, New Delhi 110 095
www.inkfeathers.com

ISBN 978-81-19483-92-1

MINDFUL PRODUCTIVITY

How to Achieve More by Doing Less

PRANAV PANDYA

Inkfeathers Publishing
www.inkfeathers.com

AUTHOR'S NOTE

We live in a world where "busy" has become a status symbol. We pride ourselves on how much we can accomplish in a day and wear our stress and exhaustion like a badge of honour. But what if I told you there's a better way to work and live? A way that allows you to be productive and successful without sacrificing your mental and physical well-being.

That's the message of "Mindful Productivity: How to Achieve More by Doing Less." In this book, I share practical strategies for getting more done in less time while prioritizing self-care and mindfulness, which is described as simply maintaining a moment-by-moment awareness of our thoughts, feelings, bodily sensations, and the surrounding environment through a gentle, nurturing, and non-judgmental lens. Drawing on research and personal experience, I show how mindfulness can be a powerful tool for increasing focus, reducing stress, and improving overall well-being.

What I love about this book is that it's not just about being more productive. It's about being more intentional with your time and energy so that you can achieve your goals while also taking care of yourself. As someone who has struggled with burnout and overwhelm in the past, I wish I had this book years ago. I believe it has the power to help readers transform the way they work and live.

So, if you're tired of the "busy" mentality and ready to embrace a more mindful and productive approach to life, this book is for you. I encourage you to read it with an open mind and heart and let the lessons guide you to a more fulfilling and sustainable way of working and living.

Pranav Pandya

CONTENTS

CHAPTER 1

INTRODUCTION: THE CASE FOR MINDFUL PRODUCTIVITY

We live in a world that values productivity above all else. We are constantly bombarded with messages about the importance of "hustle" and "grind" and encouraged to work harder, faster, and longer. But at what cost? For many of us, this relentless pursuit of productivity has led to burnout, stress, and a general sense of dissatisfaction with our work and lives.

What if there was a better way to approach productivity? What if we could achieve more by doing less? That's the promise of mindful productivity—a way of working and living that prioritizes focus, intentionality, and well-being.

At its core, mindful productivity is about working smarter, not harder. It's about recognizing that our time and energy are limited resources and using them most effectively and efficiently. It's about setting priorities based on our values and goals rather than simply reacting to the demands of others. And it's about being present and engaged in our work rather than distracted and overwhelmed.

But mindful productivity is more than just a productivity hack. It's a holistic approach to life that recognizes the interconnectedness of our physical, mental, and emotional well-being. It's about taking care of ourselves so we can show up as our best selves in our work and relationships.

In this book, we'll explore the principles and practices of mindful productivity, drawing on research and personal experience to show how it can transform the way we work and live. We'll cover topics such as time management, task prioritization, energy management, communication, mindset, habits, and leadership and provide practical strategies for implementing mindful productivity in your own life.

Ultimately, this book is about empowering you to create a more fulfilling and sustainable work and life balance. It's about helping you achieve your goals and aspirations without sacrificing your well-being.

It's about embracing a new way of thinking about productivity that is both effective and compassionate.

So, whether you're a busy professional, a student, an entrepreneur, or anyone who wants to achieve more by doing less, this book is for you. Let's embark on this journey of mindful productivity together and create a more fulfilling and sustainable way of working and living.

THE PROBLEMS WITH TRADITIONAL PRODUCTIVITY APPROACHES

For many of us, traditional productivity approaches involve working harder and longer, sacrificing our time and energy to meet deadlines and complete tasks. We are encouraged to prioritize efficiency and output over quality and creativity and often find ourselves struggling to keep up with the demands of our work.

But this approach to productivity comes with a host of problems. For one, it can lead to burnout, stress, and mental and physical health issues. When we are constantly working at a frenetic pace, we don't have the time or space to take care of ourselves, which can lead to fatigue, anxiety, and other negative outcomes.

Additionally, traditional productivity approaches often prioritize quantity over quality. We are encouraged to produce more, faster, and with fewer resources, which can result in shoddy work that doesn't meet our own or others' standards. This can damage our reputation and credibility and erode our sense of self-worth and purpose.

Another issue with traditional productivity approaches is that they don't take into account the unique needs and goals of each individual. We are often given one-size-fits-all solutions that don't account for our personal preferences, strengths, or limitations. This can lead to feelings of frustration and inadequacy when we aren't able to meet the expectations set by these approaches.

Finally, traditional productivity approaches can be overly focused on external measures of success, such as promotions, awards, or financial gain. While these things can be important, they don't necessarily reflect our inner sense of fulfilment and purpose. When we prioritize external validation over our sense of satisfaction and meaning, we can feel empty and unfulfilled, even when we've achieved these markers of success.

In this book, we'll explore an alternative approach to productivity that prioritizes well-being, creativity, and purpose. By adopting a mindful approach to productivity, we can achieve our goals without sacrificing our health and happiness. We'll provide practical strategies for incorporating mindfulness into our work and lives and show how it can transform the way we think about productivity and success.

THE BENEFITS OF MINDFULNESS FOR PRODUCTIVITY AND WELL-BEING

Mindfulness is a state of focused awareness of the present moment without judgment or distraction. It's an ancient practice that has been used for thousands of years to cultivate a sense of inner peace and well-being. But in recent years, mindfulness has gained attention in the Western world as a way to boost productivity and achieve success.

The benefits of mindfulness for productivity and well-being are numerous. For one, mindfulness helps us to stay focused and present in the moment, which can improve our ability to complete tasks and meet deadlines. When fully engaged in what we're doing, we're less likely to make mistakes or overlook important details, which can save time and reduce stress.

Additionally, mindfulness can help us to manage our emotions and reactions to stressful situations. When we're stressed or overwhelmed, our brains go into "fight or flight" mode, which can impair our ability to think clearly and make good decisions. But when we practice mindfulness, we learn to recognize and regulate our emotions, which can help us stay calm and focused under pressure.

Another benefit of mindfulness for productivity and well-being is that it can improve our overall health and happiness. Mindfulness has been shown to reduce stress, anxiety, and depression. It can improve our immune system, sleep quality, and overall sense of well-being. When we're healthy and happy, we're more likely to be productive and successful in all areas of our lives.

Finally, mindfulness can help us to cultivate a sense of purpose and meaning in our work and lives. By staying connected to our values and goals, we can create work that is meaningful and fulfilling rather than simply focusing on external markers of success. This can improve our sense of satisfaction and motivation and help us stay committed to our work and goals over the long term.

In this book, we'll explore the various ways that mindfulness can benefit our productivity and well-being and provide practical strategies for incorporating mindfulness into our work and lives. Whether you're a busy professional, a student, or anyone looking to achieve more while staying healthy and happy, we will also show you how mindfulness can help you achieve your goals and live a more fulfilling life.

WHAT TO EXPECT FROM THE BOOK

In this book, we'll explore an alternative approach to productivity that prioritizes mindfulness, well-being, and purpose. We'll begin by examining the problems with traditional productivity approaches and why they often lead to burnout, stress, and dissatisfaction. From there, we'll delve into the benefits of mindfulness for productivity and well-being and show how it can transform the way we work and live.

Throughout the book, we'll provide practical strategies for incorporating mindfulness into our work and lives. We'll explore mindfulness techniques for staying focused and present in the moment, managing stress and emotions, and cultivating a sense of purpose and meaning in our work. We'll also provide tips for creating a mindful work environment, building supportive relationships with colleagues and mentors, and setting realistic goals and expectations.

In addition to practical strategies, we'll share personal stories and case studies from individuals who have successfully integrated mindfulness into their work and lives. These stories will provide inspiration and guidance for readers who may be struggling to incorporate mindfulness into their own lives.

By the end of the book, readers can expect to have a deeper understanding of how mindfulness can improve their productivity and well-being and practical tools and strategies for incorporating mindfulness into their daily lives. They'll also have a greater sense of purpose and meaning in their work and a renewed sense of motivation and energy for achieving their goals.

Whether you're a busy professional, a student, or anyone looking to achieve more while staying healthy and happy, this book will provide you with the tools and guidance you need to achieve your goals and live a more fulfilling life. So, let's get started on our journey toward mindful productivity and well-being!

CHAPTER 2

MINDFUL TIME MANAGEMENT

Time management is a critical skill for productivity and success. Still, traditional time management approaches can often leave us feeling overwhelmed and stressed. In this chapter, we'll explore how mindfulness can transform the way we approach time management and provide practical strategies for managing our time in a mindful way.

First, we'll examine the problems with traditional time management approaches, such as rigid schedules and to-do lists, and why they can often lead to burnout and stress. We'll show how mindfulness can help us stay focused and present in the moment and create a more flexible and adaptable approach to time management.

Next, we'll explore practical strategies for incorporating mindfulness into our time management practices. We'll show how mindfulness can help us prioritize our tasks and activities, stay focused on the present moment, and avoid distractions and procrastination. We'll also provide tips for setting realistic goals and expectations and creating a more balanced and sustainable approach to time management.

Throughout the chapter, we'll provide real-life examples and case studies of individuals who have successfully integrated mindfulness into their time management practices. We'll share their stories and insights and provide practical tips and strategies for readers who may be struggling with time management issues.

By the end of the chapter, readers can expect to have a deeper understanding of how mindfulness can transform the way they approach time management and practical tools and strategies for managing their time in a more mindful and effective way.

They'll also have a greater sense of clarity and focus and a renewed sense of energy and motivation for achieving their goals.

Whether you're a busy professional, a student, or anyone looking to improve their time management skills while staying healthy and happy, this chapter will provide you with the guidance and inspiration you need to achieve your goals and live a more fulfilling life. So, let's dive into the world of prudent time management and start transforming the way we work and live!

HOW TO SET PRIORITIES AND GOALS BASED ON YOUR VALUES

One of the key benefits of incorporating mindfulness into our time management practices is that it helps us align our priorities and goals with our values. When we're mindful, we're better able to reflect on what's truly important to us and make decisions that are in line with our values and purpose.

In this section, we'll explore how to set priorities and goals based on your values. We'll begin by examining why it's important to align our priorities and goals with our values and how this can help us stay motivated and focused.

Next, we'll provide practical strategies for identifying our values and using them to set priorities and goals. We'll show how mindfulness can help us tune into our inner wisdom and intuition and provide exercises and techniques for reflecting on our values and identifying our top priorities.

Once we've identified our values and priorities, we'll explore how to use them to set realistic and achievable goals. We'll provide tips for breaking down larger goals into smaller, more manageable steps and show how to use mindfulness to stay focused and present at the moment while working towards our goals.

Throughout this section, we'll provide real-life examples and case studies of individuals who have successfully aligned their priorities and goals with their values. We'll share their stories and insights and provide practical tips and strategies for readers who may be struggling with setting priorities and goals.

By the end of this section, readers can expect to have a deeper understanding of how to set priorities and goals based on their values and practical tools and strategies for aligning their time management practices with their values and purpose.

They'll also have a greater sense of clarity and focus and a renewed sense of energy and motivation for achieving their goals in a mindful and sustainable way.

Whether you're a busy professional, a student, or anyone looking to improve your time management skills while staying true to your values, this section will provide you with the guidance and inspiration you need to achieve your goals and live a more fulfilling life. So, let's get started on our journey toward mindful time management and goal setting based on our values!

Here are a few examples and case studies of individuals who have successfully aligned their priorities and goals with their values:

Mary: Mary is a busy working mother who struggles to balance her work and personal life. She felt like she was constantly running from one task to another and never had time to focus on what was truly important to her. Through mindfulness practices, Mary was able to identify her core values, such as family, health, and personal growth. She then used these values to set priorities and goals that aligned with her values, such as spending more quality time with her family, exercising regularly, and pursuing hobbies that brought her joy. By aligning her priorities and goals with her values, Mary was able to create a more fulfilling and balanced life that allowed her to thrive both personally and professionally.

John: John is an entrepreneur who struggled with burnout and stress due to his demanding work schedule. Through mindfulness practices, John was able to identify his core values, such as creativity, innovation, and making a positive impact on the world. He then used these values to set priorities and goals that aligned with his values, such as carving out time for creative thinking and pursuing projects that aligned with his values. By aligning his priorities and goals with his values, John was able to create a more sustainable and fulfilling work-life balance that allowed him to be more productive and innovative in his work.

Sarah: Sarah is a student who struggles with procrastination and feels overwhelmed with her coursework. Through mindfulness practices, Sarah was able to identify her core values, such as learning, personal growth, and making a positive impact on the world. She then used these values to set priorities and goals that aligned with her values, such as dedicating time each day to studying, taking breaks to engage in self-care activities, and getting involved in extracurricular activities that aligned with her values. By aligning her priorities and goals with her values, Sarah was able to reduce her stress and anxiety and achieve academic success while also pursuing her passions and values.

These examples show how aligning priorities and goals with our values can lead to a more fulfilling and balanced life and how mindfulness practices can help us achieve this alignment. By identifying our core values and using them to guide our priorities and goals, we can create a more intentional and purposeful approach to time management that allows us to thrive personally and professionally.

TIME BLOCKING AND OTHER TECHNIQUES FOR MANAGING YOUR SCHEDULE.

Time blocking is a time management technique that involves breaking your day into blocks of time dedicated to specific tasks or activities. This technique can be particularly useful for individuals who struggle with procrastination or who have a hard time staying focused on one task for an extended period of time.

To implement time blocking, start by identifying the tasks or activities you need to complete throughout the day. Then, assign specific blocks of time to each task or activity, making sure to include breaks and time for self-care. During each time block, focus solely on the assigned task or activity, minimizing distractions and interruptions.

Other time management techniques that can be useful include:

1. Pomodoro Technique: This technique involves breaking your work into 25-minute intervals, followed by a 5-minute break. After four intervals, take a longer break of 15-20 minutes. This technique can help improve focus and productivity by providing structured work periods and frequent breaks.

2. Eisenhower Matrix: This technique involves prioritizing tasks based on their urgency and importance. Tasks are categorized into four quadrants: urgent and important, important but not urgent, urgent but not important, and not urgent or important. This technique can help individuals prioritize their tasks and make more strategic use of their time.

3. Task Batching: This technique involves grouping similar tasks and completing them in a designated time frame. For example, rather than responding to emails throughout the day, schedule a specific time to check and respond to emails. This technique can help minimize distractions and improve productivity.

By using techniques such as time blocking, the Pomodoro technique, the Eisenhower Matrix, and Task Batching, individuals can manage their time more effectively and efficiently. By minimizing distractions and staying focused on priorities, individuals can increase productivity and reduce stress, ultimately leading to a more fulfilling and balanced life.

TIPS FOR AVOIDING DISTRACTIONS AND STAYING FOCUSED.

In today's world, distractions are everywhere, from social media notifications to coworkers stopping by your desk to chat. Distractions can derail your productivity and make it challenging to manage your time effectively. However, there are techniques and tips you can use to avoid distractions and stay focused.

1. Set Boundaries: Create boundaries for yourself and communicate them to others. Let coworkers know when you need uninterrupted time to focus and turn off notifications on your phone or computer during these times.

2. Find a Quiet Space: If possible, find a quiet space to work where you won't be distracted by background noise. This could be a private office, a quiet coffee shop, or a library.

3. Use Noise-cancelling Headphones: If you can't find a quiet space, noise-cancelling headphones can help reduce background noise and create a more focused environment.

4. Prioritize Tasks: Prioritize tasks based on their urgency and importance and focus on completing the most critical tasks first. This will help you avoid getting sidetracked by less important tasks.

5. Take Breaks: Taking regular breaks can help refresh your mind and reduce the likelihood of getting distracted. Use these breaks to stretch, meditate, or take a short walk.

6. Use Tools to Minimize Distractions: There are tools available that can help minimize distractions, such as website blockers and distraction-free writing apps. Use these tools to help you stay focused on the task at hand.

7. Practice Mindfulness: Mindfulness is the practice of being present and fully engaged in the moment. By practising mindfulness, you can train your mind to stay focused and avoid distractions.

By using these techniques and tips, you can minimize distractions and stay focused on your priorities, ultimately leading to increased productivity and a more balanced life.

CHAPTER 3

MINDFUL TASK MANAGEMENT

Task management is a critical component of productivity and time management. It involves setting priorities, breaking down tasks into manageable steps, and allocating time and resources effectively. However, in today's fast-paced world, it can be easy to get overwhelmed by the number of tasks on your to-do list, leading to stress, anxiety, and a feeling of being constantly busy but not getting anything done.

Mindful task management offers a solution to this problem. It involves approaching your tasks with a calm and focused mindset, bringing awareness and intention to each task, and staying present and engaged while completing them. By practising mindful task management, you can not only increase your productivity and efficiency but also reduce stress and anxiety, leading to a more balanced and fulfilling life.

In this chapter, we will explore techniques and strategies for practising mindful task management. We will start by examining the importance of identifying and prioritizing tasks based on their urgency and importance. We will then explore techniques for breaking down tasks into manageable steps and allocating time and resources effectively. Finally, we will examine how mindfulness can be used to stay focused and present while completing tasks and how it can help you maintain a sense of calm and balance throughout your day.

Whether you are a busy professional, a student, or someone who simply wants to manage your tasks more effectively, this chapter will provide you with practical tools and strategies for practising mindful task management. By incorporating these techniques into your daily routine, you can achieve greater productivity, reduce stress and anxiety, and ultimately lead a more balanced and fulfilling life.

STRATEGIES FOR BREAKING DOWN LARGER PROJECTS INTO MANAGEABLE TASKS.

Breaking down larger projects into manageable tasks is an essential aspect of mindful task management. When faced with a complex project, it can be overwhelming to think about all the work that needs to be done. This can lead to procrastination, anxiety, and a sense of being stuck.

To avoid this—it's essential to break down larger projects into smaller, more manageable tasks. This approach allows you to focus on one task at a time, giving you a sense of progress and accomplishment as you complete each task.

There are several strategies for breaking down larger projects into manageable tasks.

One approach is starting with the end goal in mind, and working backwards is a strategy that can help you break down larger projects into manageable tasks. This approach involves identifying the outcome you want to achieve and then working backwards to identify the steps needed to get there.

To use this approach, start by defining your end goal. What is the outcome you want to achieve? This could be completing a major project, launching a new product, or achieving a personal goal.

Once you have identified your end goal, work backwards to identify the steps needed to achieve it. For example, if your end goal is to launch a new product, you might identify the following steps:

1. **Identify the target audience.**
2. **Conduct market research.**
3. **Develop the product.**
4. **Conduct test marketing.**
5. **Launch the product.**

Next, break down each step into smaller, more manageable tasks. For example, under "Develop the product," you might include tasks such as "Create a product roadmap," "Develop a prototype," and "Test the product."

Continue this process until you have identified all the tasks needed to achieve your end goal. Then, prioritize the tasks based on their importance and urgency, and start working on them one at a time.

By starting with the end goal in mind and working backwards, you'll be able to break down larger projects into smaller, more manageable tasks. This approach can help you stay focused, motivated, and on track to achieving your goals.

Another approach is to break down the project into phases or stages. Identify the major milestones or deliverables for each phase and then break them down into smaller tasks.

Breaking down a larger project into phases or stages can make it easier to manage and help you stay focused on your end goal. Each phase or stage can be thought of as a mini project with its own set of milestones and deliverables.

To break down a project into phases or stages, start by identifying the major milestones or deliverables for each phase. These are the key outcomes that you want to achieve for each stage of the project. For example, if you're working on a website redesign project, your phases might include:

- Planning Phase: Develop a project plan, identify website goals, and determine the target audience.
- Design Phase: Create website wireframes, design mockups, and finalize the design.
- Development Phase: Code the website, implement features and test functionality.
- Launch Phase: Deploy the website, promote the launch, and monitor website performance.

Once you have identified the major milestones or deliverables for each phase, break them down into smaller, more manageable tasks. For example, under the Planning Phase, you might include tasks such as "Conduct market research," "Define project scope," and "Develop a timeline."

Continue breaking down each phase into smaller tasks until you have a complete list of all the tasks needed to complete the project. Prioritize the tasks based on their importance and urgency and start working on them one at a time.

By breaking down a project into phases or stages and identifying the major milestones or deliverables for each phase, you can stay organized and focused on achieving your goals. This approach can also help you manage your time more effectively and ensure that you're making progress toward your end goal.

Finally, you can use a mind mapping or brainstorming technique to generate a list of all the tasks required for the project. Then, group related tasks together and prioritize them based on their importance and urgency.

Mind mapping or brainstorming techniques can be useful for generating a list of all the tasks required for a project. These techniques involve visualizing all the tasks needed to complete the project and grouping related tasks.

To use mind mapping or brainstorming for task management, start by writing the project's main goal in the centre of a piece of paper or a digital mind mapping tool. Then, brainstorm all the tasks needed to achieve that goal and write them down around the main goal.

Next, group related tasks together based on their similarities. For example, if you're working on a website redesign project, you might group all the tasks related to designing the homepage together. This can help you identify any tasks that are duplicative or overlapping and eliminate unnecessary work.

Once you have grouped related tasks, prioritize them based on their importance and urgency. You can use a matrix to help you prioritize tasks based on their importance and urgency, such as the Eisenhower matrix, which categorizes tasks into four quadrants based on their importance and urgency.

By using mind mapping or brainstorming techniques to generate a list of all the tasks required for a project and grouping related tasks together, you can ensure that you're not missing any key tasks and that you're approaching the project in a systematic and organized way. This approach can also help you prioritize tasks based on their importance and urgency, which can help you manage your time more effectively and ensure that you're making progress toward your end goal.

Regardless of the approach you choose, the key is to break the project down into small, manageable tasks that can be completed in a reasonable amount of time. By doing so, you'll be able to stay focused and motivated, avoid feeling overwhelmed, and ultimately achieve your goals more effectively.

HOW TO PRIORITIZE TASKS BASED ON URGENCY AND IMPORTANCE

Effective task management involves prioritizing tasks based on their urgency and importance. This can help you manage your time more effectively and ensure that you're making progress towards your goals.

One approach to prioritizing tasks is to use the Eisenhower matrix, which categorizes tasks into four quadrants based on their importance and urgency:

- **Quadrant 1: Urgent and important tasks**
- **Quadrant 2: Important but not urgent tasks**
- **Quadrant 3: Urgent but not important tasks**
- **Quadrant 4: Not urgent and not important tasks**

Quadrant 1 tasks are the most urgent and important and should be tackled first. These are typically tasks that require immediate attention and have significant consequences if they are not completed on time. Examples might include responding to urgent emails, handling customer complaints, or meeting a pressing deadline.

Quadrant 2 tasks are important but not urgent. These tasks should be given priority after Quadrant 1 tasks have been completed. Examples might include long-term projects, strategic planning, or professional development.

Quadrant 3 tasks are urgent but not important. These tasks should be delegated or deferred, if possible. Examples might include routine administrative tasks, interruptions, or low-priority meetings.

Quadrant 4 tasks are not urgent and not important. These tasks should be eliminated or minimized as much as possible. Examples might include unproductive habits, distractions, or time-wasting activities.

To prioritize tasks based on urgency and importance, start by identifying all the tasks that need to be completed. Then, categorize each task into one of the four quadrants based on its urgency and importance.

Once you have categorized the tasks, focus on completing the tasks in Quadrant 1 first, followed by tasks in Quadrant 2. Delegate or defer tasks in Quadrant 3 as much as possible and eliminate or minimize tasks in Quadrant 4.

Remember that priorities can shift over time, so it's important to regularly review and adjust your task list based on changing circumstances and new priorities. By prioritizing tasks based on their urgency and importance, you can ensure that you're making progress toward your goals and managing your time effectively.

Let us further explore other ways how to prioritize tasks based on urgency and importance:

Using the ABCDE Method: This technique involves categorizing tasks into five categories based on their priority. Tasks labelled "A" are the most important and must be completed that day. Tasks labelled "B" should be completed within the next few days, while tasks labelled "C" can be completed in the next week. Tasks labelled "D" can be delegated to someone else, and tasks labelled "E" can be eliminated.

For example, if you have a meeting with a client (A), a follow-up email to send (B), a team meeting to attend (C), a task that can be delegated to a colleague (D), and a non-essential task to eliminate (E), you will prioritize the meeting with the client over the other tasks.

Using a Ranking System: This technique involves assigning a score to each task based on urgency and importance. For example, you could give urgent tasks a score of 3 and important tasks a score of 2. Tasks that are neither urgent nor important would receive a score of 0. You would then add up the scores for each task and prioritize them based on their total score.

For example, if you have a project deadline approaching (urgent and important) and a meeting with a colleague (important but not urgent), you will assign a score of 3 to the project and a score of 2 to the meeting. The project would receive a total score of 3, while the meeting would receive a total score of 2, and you would prioritize the project over the meeting.

These are just a few examples of how to prioritize tasks based on urgency and importance. It's important to find a method that works best for you and your specific situation.

THE BENEFITS OF BATCHING SIMILAR TASKS AND MINIMIZING TASK-SWITCHING

Batching similar tasks is a productivity technique that involves grouping similar tasks and completing them in one go. This approach has several benefits, including reducing the time and mental energy required to switch between tasks, increasing focus and efficiency, and enabling a sense of momentum and accomplishment.

One of the primary benefits of batching tasks is that it reduces task-switching. Task-switching, also known as context switching, occurs when we move between different tasks or projects. Each time we switch tasks, our brain needs to adjust to the new context and reorient itself to the new task. This switching process can take time and energy and can ultimately reduce our productivity.

By batching similar tasks together, we can minimize task-switching and reduce the amount of time and energy required to shift between different types of work. For example, if you need to respond to several emails, make phone calls, and write reports, you can group all the email responses, then move onto making phone calls, and finish by writing reports. This way, you are able to minimize the time and mental energy required to switch between different types of work.

When we batch similar tasks, we can enter a flow state, which is a mental state of being fully immersed and focused on a task, often leading to increased productivity and creativity. A feeling of intense concentration, timelessness, and a sense of enjoyment in the task at hand characterizes flow.

An executive benefits from entering a flow state by batching similar tasks and minimizing task-switching. For example, an executive might batch similar tasks such as reviewing reports, answering emails, and scheduling meetings. By grouping these tasks and setting aside dedicated blocks of time to focus solely on them, the executive can enter a flow state where they are fully immersed in the task at hand and able to make progress more efficiently.

In this state, the executive can stay focused on one task for an extended period, allowing them to work through complex problems and make important decisions with a clear and uncluttered mind. For instance, an executive might spend an uninterrupted hour reviewing financial reports. During this time, they are fully absorbed in the task and able to gain a deeper understanding of the company's financial situation.

By reducing the amount of time spent switching between different types of work, an executive can also minimize distractions and interruptions, which can lead to increased productivity and a greater sense of accomplishment. Overall, entering a flow state can help executives to accomplish more in less time, reduce stress, and feel more satisfied with their work.

Another example would be a writer batching similar tasks, such as researching, outlining, and writing. By doing so, they can enter a flow state where they are fully focused on the writing process, and the words seem to flow effortlessly.

Similarly, a graphic designer may enter a flow state while working on a series of design projects, where they are fully immersed in the creative process, and the ideas seem to come naturally.

By minimizing task-switching and batching similar tasks, we can reduce the cognitive load of constantly switching between different types of work and allow ourselves to fully engage with the task at hand. This can lead to increased productivity, creativity, and satisfaction with our work.

Finally, batching tasks can create a sense of momentum and accomplishment. When we complete a batch of similar tasks, we feel a sense of progress and achievement, which can help to motivate us and keep us moving forward. This momentum can also help to reduce procrastination and increase our overall productivity.

In summary, batching similar tasks is a powerful productivity technique that can help to minimize task-switching, increase focus and efficiency, and create a sense of momentum and accomplishment. By grouping similar tasks and completing them in one go, we can work more effectively and efficiently and ultimately achieve our goals more quickly and easily.

CHAPTER 4

MINDFUL ENERGY MANAGEMENT

Managing our energy is crucial to achieving optimal productivity and well-being. Many of us focus solely on managing our time but neglect the importance of managing our energy levels. This chapter will explore the concept of mindful energy management, including the benefits of doing so and practical strategies to implement in daily life.

Understanding the Four Dimensions of Energy: Energy is not a one-dimensional concept. In order to manage our energy effectively, we need to understand the four dimensions of energy - physical, emotional, mental, and spiritual. Each of these dimensions plays a role in our overall energy levels, and they are all interconnected. In this section, we will delve deeper into each of these dimensions, exploring what they are, how they impact our energy, and how to manage them mindfully.

STRATEGIES FOR PHYSICAL ENERGY MANAGEMENT

Physical energy is a critical aspect of our overall well-being and productivity. When we neglect our physical health, it can lead to fatigue, decreased motivation, and reduced cognitive function. Therefore, it is essential to manage our physical energy effectively.

One important factor in managing physical energy is maintaining a healthy diet. Additionally, it is important to stay hydrated throughout the day by drinking plenty of water.

Healthy Diet:

Eating a healthy and balanced diet is essential for maintaining physical energy throughout the day. This means consuming a variety of whole foods, including fruits, vegetables, whole grains, lean proteins, and healthy fats. It's important to limit processed foods, sugary drinks, and alcohol, as these can lead to energy crashes and fatigue.

Additionally, making sure to eat breakfast and snack on healthy options throughout the day can help maintain stable energy levels.

Staying Hydrated:

Dehydration can lead to fatigue and decreased mental and physical performance, so it's important to stay hydrated throughout the day. Drinking water is the best option, but other hydrating beverages like herbal tea or coconut water can also be beneficial. Aim for at least 8 cups of water per day, and more if you're physically active or live in a hot climate. Keep a water bottle with you throughout the day as a reminder to stay hydrated.

Regular Exercise:

Regular exercise is another important strategy for managing physical energy. Exercise has been shown to have numerous physical and mental health benefits, including increased energy levels, improved cardiovascular health, and reduced stress and anxiety.

To incorporate exercise into your daily routine—it's important to find an activity that you enjoy—and that fits into your schedule. This could be anything from taking a daily walk, joining a gym, participating in a team sport, or what is now increasingly popular, practising Yoga, where scientific evidence shows that Yoga supports stress management, mental health, mindfulness, healthy eating, weight loss, and quality sleep.

The key is to make exercise a regular part of your routine.

It's also important to set realistic goals for yourself and to gradually increase the intensity and duration of your workouts. If you're new to exercise or have any health concerns, it's a good idea to consult with a healthcare professional before starting a new exercise program.

In addition to structured exercise, it's important to stay active throughout the day. This could mean taking the stairs instead of the elevator, going for a walk during your lunch break, or doing some stretching or light exercises at your desk.

Remember, regular exercise is not only good for your physical health but also for your mental and emotional well-being. Incorporating physical activity into your daily routine can help boost your energy levels and improve your overall quality of life.

Getting Enough Quality Sleep:

Getting enough quality sleep is an essential aspect of physical energy management. Good sleep helps to restore and rejuvenate the body, allowing you to wake up feeling refreshed and energized. Here are some strategies for improving sleep quality:

1. **Stick to a regular sleep schedule:** Go to bed and wake up at the same time every day, even on weekends. This helps to regulate your body's internal clock and improve the quality of your sleep.
2. **Create a relaxing sleep environment:** Make sure your bedroom is quiet, cool, and dark. Use comfortable bedding

and a supportive mattress to create a comfortable sleep environment.

3. **Limit screen time before bed:** The blue light emitted by electronic devices can disrupt sleep by interfering with the production of melatonin, a hormone that regulates sleep. Avoid using electronic devices for at least an hour before bed.
4. **Practice a relaxing bedtime routine:** Develop a relaxing bedtime routine to help you unwind and prepare for sleep. This could include reading a book, taking a warm bath, or practising relaxation techniques such as deep breathing or meditation.
5. **Avoid stimulants before bed:** Avoid caffeine, nicotine, and alcohol before bed, as they can interfere with sleep quality.
6. **Address any sleep disorders:** If you have trouble sleeping or suspect you may have a sleep disorder, such as sleep apnea or restless leg syndrome, talk to your doctor. Treating these conditions can improve the quality of your sleep and overall physical energy.

By prioritizing healthy eating, regular exercise, and quality sleep, we can effectively manage our physical energy and improve our overall well-being and productivity.

STRATEGIES FOR EMOTIONAL ENERGY MANAGEMENT

Emotional energy management is all about managing our emotions and cultivating a positive mindset. This involves recognizing and regulating our emotions, building positive relationships, and finding ways to cultivate joy and fulfilment in our lives. Here are some strategies for managing emotional energy:

Practice Self-awareness:

Self-awareness is a key strategy for managing emotional energy effectively. It involves being able to recognize and understand our own emotions and how they impact our thoughts and actions. By becoming more self-aware, we can identify triggers that may lead to emotional stress or exhaustion and take steps to prevent or manage them.

One way to practice self-awareness is to take time for self-reflection. This can involve journaling, meditation, or simply taking a few moments each day to reflect on our emotions and how we are feeling. It's also helpful to pay attention to our physical sensations, such as tension in the body or changes in breathing, which can be signs of emotional stress.

Another important aspect of self-awareness is learning to recognize our limits and boundaries.

This means being able to say no when we need to and setting boundaries around our time and energy. It can also involve taking regular breaks throughout the day to recharge and prevent burnout.

Finally, practising self-compassion is an important component of self-awareness. This means treating ourselves with kindness and understanding when we make mistakes or face challenges. By being kind and compassionate with ourselves, we can reduce the emotional toll of stress and better manage our emotional energy.

Build Positive Relationships:

Building positive relationships is another strategy that can help us manage our emotional energy effectively. Positive relationships provide us with a support system and can help us feel happier and more fulfilled in our personal and professional lives.

To build positive relationships—it's important to start by focusing on effective communication. This means being an active listener, showing empathy, and being open and honest in our interactions with others. It's also important to show appreciation and gratitude for the people in our lives and to take the time to build and maintain these relationships.

Another way to build positive relationships is to seek out common interests or activities with others. This can help to create a sense of shared experience and can lead to stronger, more meaningful relationships.

It's also important to be mindful of the types of relationships we cultivate in our lives. Surrounding ourselves with positive, supportive people can have a significant impact on our emotional energy and overall well-being. Conversely, negative or toxic relationships can drain our energy and leave us feeling drained or unhappy.

By being intentional about the relationships we build and nurture in our lives, we can help to boost our emotional energy and lead a more fulfilling, satisfying life.

Cultivate Gratitude:

Cultivating gratitude is an important strategy for managing emotional energy. When we focus on the positive aspects of our lives and appreciate the good things we have, we create a sense of contentment and happiness that can help us manage stress and negative emotions.

One way to cultivate gratitude is to keep a gratitude journal, where you write down a few things each day that you are thankful for. This practice helps us focus on the good things in our lives, no matter how small they may be.

Another way to cultivate gratitude is to practice mindfulness. This involves paying attention to the present moment and being fully present in our experiences. When we are mindful, we can appreciate the beauty and wonder of the world around us, which can help us feel more grateful.

Finally, expressing gratitude to others can also help us cultivate gratitude. This can be as simple as saying thank you to someone who has done something kind for us or writing a heartfelt letter to someone we appreciate. When we express gratitude to others, we not only make them feel good, but we also create a positive feedback loop of gratitude and positivity in our own lives.

Find Purpose and Meaning:

Finding purpose and meaning in our lives can be a powerful way to boost our emotional energy. When we have a sense of purpose and meaning, we are more motivated, resilient, and able to handle stress.

To cultivate a sense of purpose and meaning—it can be helpful to reflect on our values and what is important to us. This may involve asking ourselves questions such as: What brings us joy and fulfilment? What do we want to achieve in our lives? How do we want to contribute to the world?

Once we have a sense of our values and what is important to us, we can start to set goals and take actions that align with those values. This can help us feel more engaged and motivated in our work and personal lives.

It's also important to remember that our sense of purpose and meaning can evolve over time. As we grow and change, our priorities and goals may shift. Being open to exploring new opportunities and experiences can help us continue to find purpose and meaning in our lives.

By implementing these strategies, you can effectively manage your emotional energy, leading to greater happiness, resilience, and overall well-being.

STRATEGIES FOR MENTAL ENERGY MANAGEMENT:

Strategies for Mental Energy Management can help you stay focused, think clearly, and make effective decisions. Here are some practical tips:

Prioritize Tasks:

Prioritizing tasks involves determining which tasks are most important and urgent and then allocating time and resources accordingly. One effective way to prioritize tasks is to use the Eisenhower Matrix, which categorizes tasks into four quadrants:

Urgent and important: Tasks that are both urgent and important should be tackled first, as they require immediate attention and have a significant impact on achieving our goals. For example, responding to a time-sensitive client request or completing a project deadline that is due soon.

Not urgent but important: These tasks are important but not necessarily time-sensitive, and they may require more planning and strategizing. Examples include building new client relationships or developing new business strategies. These tasks should be given high priority to ensure they get done in a timely manner.

Urgent but not important: These tasks are often reactive in nature and do not contribute to long-term goals or success. They should be delegated or eliminated whenever possible. For example, attending a meeting that is not critical or responding to non-urgent emails.

Not urgent and not important: These tasks are typically distractions that can be eliminated to increase productivity. Examples include browsing social media or checking personal email during work hours.

By using the Eisenhower Matrix, individuals can prioritize their tasks effectively and focus on those that are most critical to achieving their goals while minimizing distractions and time-wasting activities. It's important to regularly review and update task priorities as circumstances change and new tasks arise.

Take Breaks:

Taking breaks is a crucial aspect of effective mental energy management. Our brains are not designed to work continuously without rest, and taking regular breaks can actually improve productivity and focus.

One effective strategy is the Pomodoro Technique, which involves working for a focused period, typically 25 minutes, and then taking a short break before resuming work. After four Pomodoros, you can take a longer break of 15-30 minutes.

Another approach is to take a break every hour, even if it's just for a few minutes. During this time, step away from your desk, stretch, take a walk, or engage in a relaxing activity.

It's important to use break time as an opportunity to recharge your mental batteries rather than filling it with activities that can be draining or distracting, such as checking social media or email. Engage in activities that help you relax, recharge, and refocus, such as meditation, deep breathing, or visualization exercises.

By prioritizing breaks and using them effectively, you can help to maintain your mental energy throughout the day, avoid burnout, and improve your overall productivity and well-being.

Taking regular breaks can help you recharge and stay fresh throughout the day. It's important to step away from your work and take breaks that allow you to recharge your mental batteries.

Avoid Multitasking:

Multitasking is the act of juggling multiple tasks or activities simultaneously. It's a common misconception that multitasking is an efficient way to get more done in less time. However, studies have shown that multitasking can actually be counterproductive and lead to decreased productivity, increased stress levels, and decreased accuracy.

When we try to focus on multiple tasks at once, we end up switching our attention rapidly between them. This can lead to "attention residue," where our attention remains on the previous task even after we've switched to a new one, causing a decrease in focus and productivity. Additionally, trying to do too many things at once can lead to a feeling of overwhelm and stress, further decreasing our ability to be productive and efficient.

To avoid multitasking—it's important to focus on one task at a time and complete it before moving on to the next one. This allows us to give our full attention and effort to each task, leading to better results and higher-quality work. Additionally, taking breaks between tasks can help refresh our minds and prevent burnout, allowing us to return to tasks with renewed focus and energy.

Avoiding multitasking can lead to increased productivity, improved quality of work, and decreased stress levels. By focusing on one task at a time and taking breaks when needed, we can manage our mental energy more effectively and achieve our goals more efficiently.

Overall, while multitasking may seem like an efficient way to get things done, research shows that it can actually reduce productivity and increase stress levels. Instead, focus on one task at a time and give it your full attention.

Practice Mindfulness:

Practising mindfulness is an effective strategy for managing mental energy. Mindfulness is the practice of being fully present and engaged in the moment without judgment or distraction. By practising mindfulness, we can reduce stress and improve our ability to focus and concentrate.

There are several techniques for practising mindfulness, including meditation, deep breathing exercises, and body scan exercises. Meditation involves sitting quietly and focusing on the breath while allowing thoughts to come and go without judgment. Deep breathing exercises involve taking slow, deliberate breaths and focusing on the sensation of the breath as it enters and leaves the body. Body scan exercises involve focusing on the physical sensations of different parts of the body, one at a time, in order to become more aware of the body and its sensations.

In addition to formal mindfulness practices, we can also practice mindfulness in our daily lives. This involves being fully present and engaged in the tasks we are performing, whether it's working on a project, having a conversation with someone, or even washing dishes. By focusing our attention fully on the task at hand, we can reduce distractions and increase our productivity and effectiveness.

In order to incorporate mindfulness into our daily lives, it can be helpful to set reminders or cues throughout the day to bring our attention back to the present moment. For example, we can set a reminder to take a few deep breaths before starting a new task, or we can use a mindfulness app to prompt us to take a moment to check in with ourselves throughout the day.

Practising mindfulness can help us manage our mental energy more effectively by reducing stress and increasing our ability to focus and concentrate.

Overall, Mindfulness is the practice of being fully present and engaged at the moment. It can help reduce stress, increase focus, and improve decision-making. Try incorporating mindfulness practices, such as meditation or deep breathing, into your daily routine.

Manage Distractions:

Distractions can be a major drain on mental energy, and they can make it difficult to focus on tasks and get things done. To manage distractions effectively—it's important to identify the sources of distractions and find ways to minimize or eliminate them.

Here are some strategies for managing distractions:

Minimize Digital Distractions: Turn off notifications on your phone, close unnecessary tabs on your computer, and use apps like Freedom or StayFocusd to block distracting websites during work hours.

Create a focused environment: Find a quiet space to work, use noise-cancelling headphones, and minimize visual distractions by keeping your workspace tidy.

Use the Pomodoro Technique: This technique involves working in focused 25-minute intervals, followed by a 5-minute break. During the 25-minute work intervals, you focus on a single task without any interruptions or distractions.

Practice Mindfulness: When you notice a distracting thought or urge, acknowledge it and then let it go. Try not to get caught up in the distraction or judgment about yourself for being distracted.

Use a Task List: When you're working on a specific task, write down any distracting thoughts or ideas that come up, and then return to your task. This can help you feel less anxious about potentially forgetting something important while also helping you stay focused on the task at hand.

Set aside specific times to check emails and social media.

By implementing these strategies, you can reduce the impact of distractions on your mental energy and increase your ability to focus and get things done.

Learn to Say No:

Learning to say no is an important strategy for managing mental energy. It can be difficult to turn down requests or opportunities, but saying yes to everything can quickly lead to overload and burnout. Learning to say no means recognizing your limits and priorities and being willing to set boundaries to protect your time and energy.

To learn to say no effectively, it's important to first understand your priorities and goals. This means taking the time to reflect on what's important to you, both in your personal and professional life. Once you have a clear understanding of your priorities, you can use this as a guide for deciding what requests or opportunities to say yes or no to.

When considering a request, take the time to evaluate how it fits with your priorities and goals. Will it help you move closer to your desired outcomes, or will it take you off track? If it's not aligned with your priorities, it's likely a good candidate for saying no.

It's also important to remember that saying no doesn't have to be confrontational or negative. You can still be polite and respectful while declining a request. For example, you might say something like, "Thank you for thinking of me for this opportunity, but I'm not able to take on any additional commitments right now."

Learning to say no can be a difficult skill to develop, but it's essential for managing your mental energy and staying focused on your priorities.

By implementing these strategies, you can effectively manage your mental energy and stay focused and productive throughout the day.

STRATEGIES FOR SPIRITUAL ENERGY MANAGEMENT

Meditation:

Meditation is a powerful tool for spiritual energy management. It involves focusing one's attention on a particular object, thought, or activity to achieve a mentally clear and emotionally calm state. By quieting the mind and releasing distractions, meditation can help reduce stress and anxiety, increase feelings of well-being, and promote a sense of inner peace and harmony.

There are many different types of meditation, each with its unique approach and benefits. Some popular forms of meditation include mindfulness meditation, transcendental meditation, loving-kindness meditation, and yoga meditation.

To get started with meditation, find a quiet, comfortable space where you can sit or lie down without distractions. Set a timer for a few minutes to start, and gradually work your way up to longer meditation sessions. Focus your attention on your breath, a mantra, or a specific sensation in your body. When your mind wanders, gently bring your attention back to your object of focus. Over time, you may find that meditation becomes a natural and integral part of your daily routine, helping you to cultivate greater awareness, clarity, and spiritual connection.

Mindful Breathing:

Mindful breathing is a simple yet powerful technique that can be used to manage stress and improve focus. It involves intentionally focusing on the breath and noticing the physical sensations associated with breathing, such as the movement of the diaphragm and the feeling of air entering and leaving the body.

To practice mindful breathing, find a quiet place where you can sit comfortably and without distractions. Close your eyes and take a few deep breaths to help relax your body. Then, begin to breathe naturally and focus your attention on the sensation of your breath as it enters and leaves your body. You may choose to focus on the feeling of the air moving in and out of your nostrils or the rising and falling of your chest or belly.

As you focus on your breath, your mind may begin to wander. This is normal and expected. When you notice your mind wandering, simply acknowledge the thought or distraction and gently bring your attention back to your breath.

Regular practice of mindful breathing can help to reduce stress and anxiety, improve focus and concentration, and promote feelings of calm and relaxation. It can be a helpful tool for managing the demands of daily life and cultivating a sense of inner peace and well-being.

Gratitude:

Gratitude is another powerful strategy for managing spiritual energy. By cultivating gratitude, we can focus on the positive aspects of our lives rather than getting bogged down by negative thoughts and emotions. When we practice gratitude, we acknowledge the good things that we have in our lives and feel thankful for them.

There are many ways to practice gratitude, but one effective technique is to keep a gratitude journal.

This involves writing down three to five things that you are grateful for each day. These things can be big or small, but the important thing is that they are meaningful to you. By focusing on the positive aspects of your life, you can shift your mindset towards one of abundance and gratitude.

Another way to practice gratitude is to express it to others. You can tell a friend or family member how much you appreciate them or even write a thank-you note to someone who has made a positive impact on your life. By expressing gratitude to others, you can strengthen your relationships and create a positive ripple effect.

In addition, you can also practice gratitude at the moment by taking the time to appreciate the small things in life. This could be as simple as enjoying a beautiful sunset or savouring a delicious meal. By being mindful and fully present at the moment, you can cultivate a sense of gratitude and appreciation for the world around you.

Spending Time in Nature:

Spending time in nature can be a powerful strategy for spiritual energy management. Being surrounded by natural beauty can help us feel more connected to the world around us and provide a sense of peace and calm. This can be especially important in today's fast-paced, technology-driven world, where we often feel disconnected from nature.

Studies have shown that spending time in nature can have a range of benefits, including reducing stress and anxiety, improving mood and cognitive function, and increasing creativity and productivity. Even just a short walk in a park or nature reserve can be enough to provide a mental and emotional boost.

To incorporate nature into your spiritual energy management routine, try to spend some time outside every day, even if it's just a few minutes. You might take a walk in a local park or nature reserve, sit outside and enjoy a cup of tea, or simply take a few deep breaths and observe the natural world around you. You can also try incorporating nature into your home or office environment by adding plants or natural elements like wood or stone.

Additionally, activities like hiking, camping, or bird watching can provide even greater opportunities to connect with nature and reap the benefits of spending time in natural settings. By prioritizing time in nature and making it a regular part of your routine, you can help cultivate a sense of spiritual well-being and improve your overall energy management.

Engaging in Spiritual Practices:

Engaging in spiritual practices can be an effective way to manage spiritual energy. These practices can vary depending on one's personal beliefs and preferences. Here are some examples:

1. **Prayer:** Prayer can be a powerful way to connect with a higher power or deity and find spiritual guidance and comfort.
2. **Yoga:** Yoga is a physical and spiritual practice that originated in ancient India. It involves posture, breathing exercises, and meditation and can help improve physical, mental, and spiritual well-being.
3. **Meditation:** Meditation can be a secular or spiritual practice that involves focusing one's attention on the present moment and cultivating a state of calm and relaxation. It can help reduce stress and anxiety and increase feelings of peace and connectedness.
4. **Mindful journaling:** Writing down thoughts and feelings in a journal can be a way to reflect on one's spiritual journey and connect with deeper emotions and beliefs.
5. **Reading spiritual texts:** Reading texts such as religious scriptures, poetry, or philosophical writings can be a way to gain insight and inspiration and connect with a higher purpose.
6. **Volunteering and service:** Engaging in acts of service and giving back to others can be a way to connect with a sense of purpose and make a positive impact in the world.

Overall, engaging in spiritual practices can help individuals connect with their inner selves and a higher power, find meaning and purpose in life, and feel a sense of peace and fulfilment. By incorporating these strategies into your daily routine, you can help to manage your spiritual energy and promote a sense of overall well-being.

CHAPTER 5

MINDFUL COMMUNICATION

Effective communication is the cornerstone of success in both personal and professional relationships. It is a skill that can be developed and enhanced through mindful practice. Mindful communication involves being present and fully engaged in the communication process, actively listening to others, and expressing oneself in a clear, concise, and respectful manner. In this chapter, we will explore the principles of mindful communication and provide practical strategies for improving communication skills.

PRINCIPLES OF MINDFUL COMMUNICATION

Presence:

Presence is an essential aspect of mindful communication. Being present means being fully engaged and attentive to the person or people you are communicating with without distractions or preconceived notions. It involves being aware of your thoughts, feelings, and biases, as well as those of the person you are communicating with.

When you are fully present in a conversation, you are better able to listen actively and respond authentically. You can notice subtle cues such as body language and tone of voice and can more easily tune in to the emotions and needs of the person you are speaking with. This can help you build trust and rapport and create a deeper connection with the other person.

To practice presence in your communication, start by setting aside distractions such as your phone or computer. Give your full attention to the person you are communicating with, and try to remain present in the moment. Avoid interrupting or multitasking, and instead, focus on what is being said and how it is being said. Be aware of your own emotions and reactions, and try to remain calm and centred, even in difficult or challenging conversations.

By practising presence in your communication, you can improve the quality of your interactions with others, build stronger relationships, and cultivate greater empathy and understanding.

Active Listening:

Active listening is an essential aspect of mindful communication. It involves being fully present and engaged in a conversation and making a conscious effort to understand the other person's perspective. Active listening requires you to set aside your own thoughts, judgments, and biases and focus solely on the speaker's words, tone, and body language.

To practice active listening—you can start by giving the speaker your undivided attention. This means eliminating distractions and making eye contact with the speaker. You should also try to be fully present at the moment and avoid multitasking or thinking about your response while the speaker is talking. Instead, focus on the speaker's words and try to understand their point of view.

Another important aspect of active listening is asking clarifying questions. This not only shows that you are paying attention but also helps to clarify any misunderstandings and ensure that you fully understand the speaker's message. It's also helpful to provide feedback to the speaker to show that you have understood their message, such as summarizing what they have said or paraphrasing their words.

Active listening can improve the quality of your communication by reducing misunderstandings and promoting empathy and understanding. It can also improve relationships by demonstrating that you value and respect the speaker's perspective.

Non-Judgment:

Non-judgment is a crucial principle of mindful communication, and it means suspending our tendency to make judgments or assumptions about the other person's actions, motives, or intentions. This involves recognizing that everyone has their unique perspective and that we can never fully know what someone else is experiencing or feeling. By suspending judgment, we can create a safe and non-threatening space for the other person to express themselves and feel heard and understood.

One way to practice non-judgment is to become aware of our own biases and assumptions and to question them. We can also try to see the situation from the other person's point of view and empathize with their feelings and emotions rather than simply reacting based on our preconceived notions. This involves being curious and open-minded rather than closed off and defensive.

Another way to practice non-judgment is to cultivate a sense of compassion for ourselves and others. We can recognize that everyone makes mistakes and that we are all doing the best we can with the resources we have. By practising self-compassion and extending compassion to others, we can create a more supportive and understanding environment for communication to occur.

Empathy:

Empathy is the ability to understand and share the feelings of others. In mindful communication, empathy is essential for building strong relationships and resolving conflicts. It involves being present with another person, listening actively to their perspective, and trying to understand their emotions and point of view. When we practice empathy, we create a safe space for others to express themselves fully, and we open ourselves up to new perspectives and insights.

To practice empathy in communication, we need to:

1. **Listen Actively:** This involves giving the person our full attention and trying to understand their perspective without judgment or interruption. We can use reflective listening techniques such as summarizing what the person has said or asking clarifying questions to ensure that we have understood them correctly.
2. **Recognize Emotions:** Emotions play a crucial role in communication. To practice empathy, we need to be aware of the emotions that the person is expressing, both verbally and non-verbally. We can reflect on the emotions we observe, such as "It sounds like you're feeling frustrated."
3. **Validate Feelings:** Validating someone's feelings means acknowledging and accepting their emotions as valid and understandable, even if we don't necessarily agree with them. We can show validation through statements such as "I can see why you feel that way" or "That must be really difficult for you.
4. **Practice Perspective-taking:** Perspective-taking involves trying to understand someone else's point of view and imagining how they might feel in a particular situation. This can help us to develop empathy by allowing us to see things from their perspective and understand their experiences and emotions.

By practising empathy in communication, we can improve our relationships with others, enhance our understanding of different perspectives, and build a more compassionate and inclusive society.

Respect:

Respect is another important principle of mindful communication. It means treating others with dignity and showing consideration for their feelings, thoughts, and perspectives. In mindful communication, respect involves acknowledging and valuing the other person's humanity and individuality, regardless of whether or not we agree with their views or behaviour.

One way to practice respect in communication is to avoid making assumptions or judgments about the other person based on their appearance, background, or past experiences. Instead, we can listen with an open mind and seek to understand their perspective. We can also avoid interrupting or talking over the other person and refrain from using aggressive or disrespectful language or tone of voice.

Respect also means taking responsibility for our communication, including our words and actions. This involves being honest and transparent about our intentions and emotions and being willing to apologize or make amends if we unintentionally cause harm or offence.

By practising respect in communication, we can create a positive and safe environment where all parties feel valued and heard, even in difficult or contentious situations.

STRATEGIES FOR MINDFUL COMMUNICATION

Practice Mindful Listening:

Practising mindful listening is an essential part of mindful communication. Mindful listening involves actively paying attention to what the speaker is saying without distractions or judgments. It means focusing on the present moment and being fully present with the speaker.

To practice mindful listening—it's essential to create a space of mutual respect and trust between the speaker and listener. This means providing the speaker with your undivided attention and avoiding distractions such as smartphones or other interruptions. It also means listening with an open mind without jumping to conclusions or making assumptions.

One technique for practising mindful listening is to use reflective listening. Reflective listening involves paraphrasing what the speaker has said to confirm understanding and show that you're listening. It's a way to check in with the speaker and ensure that you've understood their message correctly.

Another technique for mindful listening is to listen with curiosity. This means approaching the conversation with an open mind, without preconceptions or biases. It involves asking questions to clarify your understanding rather than assuming that you already know what the speaker is saying.

Finally, it's important to listen with empathy. Empathy means understanding and sharing the feelings of the speaker. It involves putting yourself in their shoes and seeing the situation from their perspective. By listening with empathy, you can better understand the speaker's feelings and communicate more effectively.

Speak Clearly and Concisely:

Speaking clearly and concisely is an important aspect of mindful communication. When we communicate, we want to be understood and avoid miscommunication or confusion. Here are some tips for speaking clearly and concisely:

1. **Be aware of your tone:** Our tone of voice can convey a lot about how we feel about the message we are communicating.

Be aware of your tone and try to speak in a tone that is calm and respectful.

2. **Use simple language:** Use language that is clear and easy to understand. Avoid using jargon or technical terms that the listener may not be familiar with.
3. **Stay on topic:** Try to stay focused on the topic at hand and avoid going off on tangents. This can help prevent confusion and keep the conversation on track.
4. **Be mindful of your words:** Choose your words carefully and be mindful of how they may be interpreted. Avoid using language that is inflammatory or judgmental.
5. **Get to the point:** Be concise in your communication. Get to the point quickly and avoid rambling or repeating yourself.
6. **Practice active listening:** While speaking clearly and concisely is important, it is also important to actively listen to the other person. Pay attention to their verbal and nonverbal cues and respond appropriately.

By practising clear and concise communication, we can improve the chances of being understood and avoid misunderstandings that can lead to conflict or confusion.

Practice Empathy:

Practising empathy is a crucial strategy for mindful communication. Empathy is the ability to understand and share the feelings of another person. When we practice empathy, we are able to connect with others on a deeper level and build stronger relationships. Here are some ways to practice empathy in communication:

1. **Listen actively:** When someone is speaking to us, it's important to focus on what they are saying and give them our

full attention. Avoid interrupting or getting distracted by other thoughts or tasks. Try to understand their perspective by asking questions and paraphrasing what they say to ensure you have a clear understanding.

2. **Put yourself in their shoes:** Imagine yourself in the other person's situation and consider how you would feel in their place. This can help you better understand their emotions and thoughts.
3. **Use "I" statements:** When expressing yourself, use "I" statements instead of "you" statements. For example, instead of saying, "You're not listening to me," say, "I feel like my concerns are not being heard." This approach is less accusatory and helps to avoid putting the other person on the defensive.
4. **Show validation:** Validate the other person's feelings by acknowledging them and showing empathy. This can be as simple as saying, "I understand how you feel," or "That sounds difficult." Validating someone's feelings can help to build trust and rapport.

By practising empathy in communication, we can build stronger relationships and create a more positive and productive work environment.

Avoid Assumptions:

The principle of avoiding assumptions is a key aspect of mindful communication. Assumptions are often made unconsciously, and they can lead to misunderstandings and conflicts in communication.

When we assume things about others, we may be projecting our own thoughts, feelings, and beliefs onto them rather than listening to and understanding their perspective.

To avoid making assumptions—it's important to approach every conversation with an open mind and a willingness to learn. This means actively listening to the other person and seeking to understand their perspective rather than assuming that we already know what they are thinking or feeling. It also means being aware of our own biases and assumptions and questioning them before making judgments about others.

Another way to avoid assumptions is to ask clarifying questions. If we are unsure about something the other person has said, we can ask for clarification to make sure we understand their perspective. This shows respect for their viewpoint and helps to avoid misunderstandings.

By avoiding assumptions, we can create a more open and respectful dialogue with others, fostering better relationships and reducing the potential for conflict in our interactions.

Stay Calm:

Staying calm is an important principle of mindful communication. When we communicate, we may encounter situations that are emotionally charged or trigger stress, anxiety, or frustration. In such situations, it is important to stay calm and composed. Reacting impulsively or emotionally can lead to misunderstandings, hurt feelings, and damage to relationships.

Staying calm requires self-awareness and emotional regulation. It is important to recognize when we are becoming emotionally triggered and take steps to regulate our emotions before responding. This can involve taking a few deep breaths, taking a break, or using mindfulness techniques to calm our minds and emotions.

Staying calm also involves being mindful of our tone of voice and body language. Communicating in a calm and respectful manner can help to diffuse tense situations and promote effective communication.

It can also help to create a safe and respectful space for others to share their thoughts and feelings.

Overall, staying calm is an important principle of mindful communication that can promote healthy relationships and effective communication.

Give and Receive Feedback:

The principle of giving and receiving feedback is an important aspect of mindful communication. Feedback helps to ensure that communication is effective, and it provides an opportunity for both parties to learn and grow. However, giving and receiving feedback can be challenging, and it requires a mindful approach.

When giving feedback, it is important to be clear and specific. Use examples to illustrate your points and be honest but also kind and respectful. Avoid criticizing the person and instead focus on their behaviour or actions. It is also important to give feedback in a timely manner and to provide suggestions for improvement.

When receiving feedback, it is important to listen actively and non-judgmentally. Avoid becoming defensive or dismissive, and instead, try to understand the perspective of the person giving the feedback. Ask clarifying questions and seek to learn from the feedback provided. It is also important to thank the person for their feedback and to take steps to address any issues or concerns raised.

By giving and receiving feedback in a mindful manner, we can improve our communication skills and build stronger relationships with those around us.

HOW TO COMMUNICATE EFFECTIVELY AND EFFICIENTLY WITH OTHERS

Effective and efficient communication is essential for building strong relationships and achieving success in both personal and professional settings. In this section, we will explore practical strategies for communicating with others in a way that is both effective and efficient.

1. **Be Clear and Concise:** When communicating with others, it is important to be clear and concise in your message. Use simple language and avoid using technical jargon or complex terms that may confuse the listener. Use bullet points or short sentences to convey your message effectively.
2. **Listen Actively:** Active listening is a key component of effective communication. When you are engaged in a conversation with someone, make sure that you are fully present and focused on what the other person is saying. Avoid distractions and interruptions and try to understand their perspective.
3. **Be Empathetic:** Empathy is the ability to understand and share the feelings of another person. By being empathetic, you can create a more positive and productive conversation. Put yourself in the other person's shoes and try to see things from their point of view.
4. **Avoid Assumptions:** Making assumptions can lead to misunderstandings and miscommunications. Avoid assuming that you know what the other person is thinking or feeling, and instead, ask for clarification or further

explanation.

5. **Stay Calm:** When communicating with others, it is important to stay calm and composed, even in challenging situations. Take a few deep breaths and try to maintain a neutral tone of voice, even if you are feeling upset or frustrated.
6. **Give and Receive Feedback:** Feedback is a valuable tool for improving communication and building stronger relationships. When giving feedback, be specific and avoid generalizations. When receiving feedback, listen carefully and avoid becoming defensive. Use feedback as an opportunity for growth and improvement.
7. **Choose the Right Time and Place:** When communicating with others, it is important to choose the right time and place for your conversation. Avoid having important discussions in noisy or distracting environments, and choose a time when both parties are well-rested and focused.

By practising these strategies for effective and efficient communication, you can build stronger relationships, improve productivity, and achieve greater success in both your personal and professional life.

STRATEGIES FOR SETTING BOUNDARIES AND SAYING NO

Setting boundaries and saying no are important strategies for maintaining healthy relationships and reducing stress. Here are some tips on how to communicate effectively and efficiently when setting boundaries and saying no:

1. **Be clear and direct:** When setting boundaries or saying no, it's important to be clear and direct with the other person. Use clear and simple language to convey your message.
2. **Express your needs:** When setting boundaries or saying no, it's important to express your needs. Explain why you need to set this boundary or say no, and how it will benefit both you and the other person in the long run.
3. **Be respectful:** While it's important to be clear and direct, it's also important to be respectful when setting boundaries or saying no. Be mindful of the other person's feelings and be empathetic.
4. **Offer alternatives:** If you are saying no to a request, offer an alternative solution or suggest someone else who may be able to help. This shows that you are still willing to be helpful, but just not in the way they are asking.
5. **Practice saying no:** If saying no is difficult for you, practice with a friend or family member. This will help you become more comfortable with setting boundaries and saying no in real-life situations.
6. **Remember that it's okay to say no:** It's important to remember that it's okay to say no. Saying no does not make you a bad person, and it's important to prioritize your own

needs and well-being.

By following these strategies, you can communicate effectively and efficiently when setting boundaries and saying no, while maintaining healthy relationships and reducing stress.

THE ROLE OF ACTIVE LISTENING AND EMPATHY IN COMMUNICATION

Active listening and empathy are two critical components of effective communication. Active listening involves paying full attention to the person who is speaking without distractions or interruptions and demonstrating that you understand what they are saying. It involves using both verbal and nonverbal cues to show that you are engaged and interested in the conversation.

Empathy, on the other hand, involves understanding and sharing the feelings and emotions of the person you are communicating with. It involves putting yourself in their shoes and trying to see things from their perspective.

When active listening and empathy are combined, it can create a powerful connection between two people, leading to more productive and meaningful conversations. Here are some strategies for incorporating active listening and empathy into your communication:

1. **Practice attentive listening:** Give the person your full attention, maintain eye contact, and avoid distractions such as checking your phone or looking around the room.
2. **Show interest:** Demonstrate that you are interested in what they are saying by nodding your head, asking questions, and giving verbal cues such as "I see" or "I understand."
3. **Reflect on what they are saying:** Repeat back what you heard to ensure that you understand their message correctly.
4. **Respond with empathy:** Show that you understand and empathize with their feelings by acknowledging their emotions and responding in a caring and supportive way.

5. **Avoid judging:** Refrain from making assumptions or judgments about the person or their situation and focus on understanding their perspective.

By incorporating active listening and empathy into your communication, you can create a more open and supportive environment where people feel heard and valued. This can lead to better relationships and more positive outcomes in both personal and professional settings.

CHAPTER 6

MINDFUL MINDSET

A mindful mindset refers to a state of awareness and focus on the present moment without judgment or distraction. It is a way of being present and fully engaged in whatever is happening without being overwhelmed by emotions or thoughts. A mindful mindset can help us manage stress, improve our mental clarity, and enhance our overall well-being.

Here are some strategies for developing a mindful mindset:

1. Practice mindfulness meditation: One of the most effective ways to cultivate a mindful mindset is through regular meditation practice. Mindfulness meditation involves sitting quietly and observing your thoughts, emotions, and physical sensations without judgment. By regularly practising mindfulness meditation, you can become more aware of your thoughts and emotions and learn to manage them more effectively.

2. Focus on the present moment: When we focus on the present moment, we can become more aware of our surroundings and the people around us. This can help us stay focused and productive and reduce feelings of anxiety and overwhelm. To stay focused on the present moment, try taking a few deep breaths and then focusing your attention on the task at hand.

3. Cultivate gratitude: Gratitude is a powerful tool for cultivating a mindful mindset. By focusing on the things that we are grateful for, we can shift our attention away from negative thoughts and emotions and focus on the positive aspects of our lives. Try writing down three things that you are grateful for each day and take a few moments to reflect on them.

4. Embrace imperfection: Many of us have a tendency to be perfectionists, which can lead to feelings of stress and anxiety. By embracing imperfection, we can learn to let go of our need for control and focus on what we can do to improve. Try to focus on progress rather than perfection, and be kind and forgiving to yourself when things don't go as planned.

5. Practice self-compassion: Self-compassion is the practice of treating ourselves with the same kindness and understanding that we would offer to a close friend. By practising self-compassion, we can learn to be more accepting of ourselves and our imperfections and let go of feelings of self-judgment and criticism.

6. Set intentions: Setting intentions can help us stay focused and motivated and keep us on track with our goals. Try setting an intention for the day or the week and make a conscious effort to focus your attention and energy on achieving it.

7. Cultivate a growth mindset: A growth mindset is a belief that our abilities and intelligence can be developed through hard work and dedication. By cultivating a growth mindset, we can learn to embrace challenges and setbacks as opportunities for growth and learning.

Developing a mindful mindset can help us manage stress, improve our mental clarity, and enhance our overall well-being. By practising mindfulness meditation, focusing on the present moment, cultivating gratitude, embracing imperfection, practising self-compassion, setting intentions, and cultivating a growth mindset, we can develop a more mindful approach to life.

THE POWER OF POSITIVE THINKING AND SELF-TALK

The power of positive thinking and self-talk is a critical aspect of developing a mindful mindset. Positive thinking involves intentionally focusing on the good in a situation rather than the negative. It involves recognizing the strengths and positive aspects of oneself and others and reframing negative thoughts into positive ones.

Self-talk refers to the internal dialogue that goes on within a person's mind. It can be positive or negative and can have a significant impact on one's thoughts, emotions, and behaviours. Positive self-talk involves using positive, supportive language to encourage oneself and build confidence.

Research has shown that adopting a positive mindset and using positive self-talk can have numerous benefits, including increased resilience, improved well-being, and greater success in achieving goals. It can also help individuals cope with stress, anxiety, and other challenges.

Here are some strategies for developing a positive mindset and practising positive self-talk:

1. **Focus on the good:** When faced with a difficult situation, try to find the positive aspects or opportunities for growth. Focus on what you can learn from the situation and how it can make you stronger.
2. **Practice gratitude:** Take time each day to reflect on the things you are grateful for. This can help shift your focus to the positive and increase feelings of well-being.
3. **Reframe negative thoughts:** When negative thoughts arise,

try to reframe them into positive ones. For example, instead of thinking, "I can't do this," try thinking, " I haven't figured this out yet, but I will keep trying."

4. **Use positive affirmations:** Repeat positive affirmations to yourself, such as "I am capable," "I am worthy," or "I am enough." This can help boost confidence and self-esteem.
5. **Surround yourself with positivity:** Surround yourself with positive people, uplifting messages, and activities that bring you joy and happiness. This can help reinforce a positive mindset and positive self-talk.

Remember, developing a positive mindset and practising positive self-talk is a process that takes time and practice. Be patient with yourself and continue to work towards a more mindful and positive mindset.

- When facing a difficult task, instead of thinking, "I can't do this," I tell myself, "I am capable and will figure it out." This positive self-talk helps me approach the task with confidence and a solution-oriented mindset.
- When dealing with stress or anxiety, I remind myself that I have faced difficult situations before and have the strength to get through this one too. This positive self-talk helps me feel more resilient and less overwhelmed.
- When trying to improve a skill, such as public speaking, I focus on the progress I am making instead of being overly critical of myself. By recognizing and celebrating small improvements, I build confidence and motivation to keep improving.
- When feeling discouraged or demotivated, I remind myself of my values and goals. This positive self-talk helps me reconnect with my purpose and find the motivation to keep pushing forward.

HOW TO CULTIVATE A GROWTH MINDSET AND OVERCOME LIMITING BELIEFS.

Cultivating a growth mindset is essential to achieve personal growth and overcoming limiting beliefs. A growth mindset is a belief that one's abilities and intelligence can be developed through hard work, perseverance, and dedication. People with a growth mindset believe that failure is an opportunity to learn and grow rather than a reflection of their abilities. Here are some strategies for cultivating a growth mindset and overcoming limiting beliefs:

1. **Embrace challenges:** Rather than avoiding challenges, people with a growth mindset embrace them as opportunities to learn and grow. They see challenges as a chance to stretch themselves and improve their skills.
2. **Learn from failure:** Failure is a natural part of the learning process. People with a growth mindset view failure as an opportunity to learn and grow rather than as a reflection of their abilities. They use failure as a chance to reflect on what went wrong and how they can improve in the future.
3. **Focus on the process:** People with a growth mindset focus on the process of learning rather than just the outcome. They understand that learning takes time and effort, and they are willing to put in the work to achieve their goals.
4. **Practice self-compassion:** Cultivating a growth mindset requires self-compassion. People with a growth mindset are kind to themselves and understand that learning and growth take time. They practice self-care and take breaks when they need them.
5. **Surround yourself with positive influences:** Surrounding

yourself with positive influences, such as supportive friends and family members, can help you cultivate a growth mindset. These people can offer encouragement and support as you work to overcome limiting beliefs.

6. **Challenge your limiting beliefs:** Everyone has limiting beliefs that hold them back. These beliefs are often based on past experiences or negative self-talk. People with a growth mindset challenge their limiting beliefs by examining the evidence and looking for alternative explanations.

By cultivating a growth mindset and challenging limiting beliefs, you can develop the confidence and resilience needed to achieve your goals and live a fulfilling life.

THE BENEFITS OF MINDFULNESS MEDITATION AND OTHER MINDFULNESS PRACTICES

Mindfulness meditation and other mindfulness practices have been found to provide numerous benefits for individuals in various areas of life. Here are some of the benefits:

1. **Reduced stress and anxiety:** Mindfulness meditation helps to reduce stress and anxiety by helping individuals to focus on the present moment and let go of worries about the past and future.
2. **Improved focus and concentration:** Mindfulness practices help to train the mind to stay focused on the present moment, which can improve concentration and focus on various tasks.
3. **Increased self-awareness**: Mindfulness practices help individuals to become more aware of their thoughts, feelings, and bodily sensations, which can help them to better understand themselves and their behaviour.
4. **Improved emotional regulation:** Mindfulness practices help individuals to regulate their emotions more effectively by allowing them to observe their emotions without judgment and respond in a more thoughtful manner.
5. **Enhanced creativity:** Mindfulness practices can enhance creativity by helping individuals to approach problems and situations with a more open and curious mind.
6. **Better sleep:** Mindfulness practices have been found to improve sleep quality by reducing stress and anxiety levels, which can interfere with restful sleep.

7. **Increased empathy and compassion:** Mindfulness practices can enhance empathy and compassion by helping individuals to develop a more open and non-judgmental attitude towards themselves and others.

Overall, incorporating mindfulness practices into daily life can lead to a greater sense of well-being, improved relationships, and increased productivity and effectiveness in various areas of life.

CHAPTER 7

MINDFUL HABITS

Our habits play a significant role in shaping our lives. They can determine our productivity, health, happiness, and overall well-being. Therefore, it is essential to cultivate mindful habits that align with our goals and values. Mindful habits are those that promote self-awareness, self-care, and personal growth. In this chapter, we will discuss the importance of mindful habits and provide practical strategies for incorporating them into your daily routine.

SECTION 1: THE IMPORTANCE OF MINDFUL HABITS

Habits and their impact on our lives

Habits are behaviours or actions that we repeat regularly, often without even being aware of them. They can be positive or negative and can have a significant impact on our lives. Our habits shape our daily routines, influencing how we spend our time, what we eat, how we communicate, and how we think.

Positive habits can have a beneficial effect on our physical and mental health, relationships, and overall well-being. For example, regular exercise can improve our physical health, reduce stress and anxiety, and boost our mood. Eating a healthy diet can provide our body with the nutrients it needs to function properly, improve our energy levels, and support our immune system. Developing positive communication habits, such as active listening and empathetic speaking, can improve our relationships and help us connect more deeply with others.

On the other hand, negative habits can have a detrimental effect on our lives. For example, habits such as smoking, excessive alcohol consumption, and overeating can increase the risk of chronic diseases and negatively impact our physical and mental health. Negative communication habits— such as interrupting or speaking without considering others' feelings, can damage our relationships and lead to misunderstandings.

Habits are powerful because they can become automatic, requiring little conscious effort to maintain. This is why it can be difficult to break a negative habit or establish a new positive one. However, with mindfulness and intentional effort, we can change our habits and create a more fulfilling and healthy life.

BENEFITS OF MINDFUL HABITS, INCLUDING INCREASED FOCUS, PRODUCTIVITY, SELF-AWARENESS, AND WELL-BEING

Cultivating mindful habits can bring a wide range of benefits to our lives. By practising mindfulness regularly, we can improve our focus, productivity, self-awareness, and overall well-being.

Increased Focus: Mindful habits, such as meditation or mindful breathing, can help to improve our ability to focus on the tasks at hand. When we train our minds to be present in the moment, we are less likely to become distracted by external factors or racing thoughts. This can lead to improved concentration and more efficient use of our time.

Increased Productivity: Mindful habits can also lead to increased productivity. When we are more focused, we are able to work more efficiently and effectively, completing tasks in a shorter amount of time. Additionally, the increased sense of clarity and purpose that comes with practising mindfulness can help us to prioritize our tasks and make better decisions.

Increased Self-awareness: Mindfulness practices can also help us to become more self-aware. By regularly checking in with ourselves and our thoughts, we can develop a greater understanding of our emotions and behaviours. This can help us to identify patterns and habits that may be holding us back and make positive changes in our lives.

Improved Well-being: Finally, mindful habits can lead to improved overall well-being. By reducing stress and increasing self-awareness, we can improve our mental health and emotional well-being. Additionally, practices like yoga or mindful movement can improve physical health and increase our sense of vitality and energy.

Cultivating mindful habits can have a profound impact on our lives. By incorporating mindfulness into our daily routines, we can improve our focus, productivity, self-awareness, and well-being.

HOW MINDFULNESS CAN ENHANCE OUR ABILITY TO DEVELOP AND MAINTAIN MINDFUL HABITS

Mindfulness is a powerful tool that can help us develop and maintain mindful habits. When we are mindful, we are fully present in the moment, aware of our thoughts, feelings, and sensations without judgment. This awareness can help us identify the habits that are not serving us and develop new habits that support our well-being and goals.

To begin—mindfulness can help us become more aware of our thoughts and emotions. By noticing our thoughts and feelings without judgment, we can better understand our habits and what triggers them. For example, if we tend to reach for a sugary snack when we are feeling stressed, mindfulness can help us identify the trigger (stress) and develop a new, healthier habit (e.g., taking a short walk, doing some deep breathing exercises, or drinking a glass of water).

In addition, mindfulness can help us stay focused on our goals and values. When we are mindful, we are better able to prioritize our time and energy, which can help us develop and maintain habits that align with our values and goals. For example, if we value our health and fitness, mindfulness can help us stay focused on exercise and healthy eating habits, even when faced with temptation or obstacles.

Finally, mindfulness can help us build resilience and self-compassion, which are key components of maintaining any habit. When we practice mindfulness, we learn to accept ourselves and our imperfections, which can help us stay motivated and committed to our habits even when we experience setbacks or challenges. By cultivating a mindful attitude of self-compassion and non-judgment, we can also overcome the negative self-talk that often sabotages our efforts to develop and maintain healthy habits.

Overall, mindfulness can be a powerful tool for developing and maintaining mindful habits. By cultivating awareness, focus, resilience, and self-compassion, we can create lasting change and live our best lives.

SECTION 2: STRATEGIES FOR CULTIVATING MINDFUL HABITS

Start with Small Changes: Make gradual adjustments to your daily routine to avoid being overwhelmed and build momentum.

When it comes to cultivating mindful habits, starting with small changes can be an effective strategy. Making gradual adjustments to your daily routine can help you avoid feeling overwhelmed and build momentum toward more significant changes.

For example, if you want to start a daily meditation practice, instead of committing to an hour-long session right away, start with just a few minutes each day. This can help you establish a consistent routine without feeling like you have to dedicate a lot of time and energy all at once.

Similarly, if you want to improve your diet, start by making small changes to your meals rather than trying to overhaul your entire eating habits all at once. Perhaps you can start by adding more vegetables to your plate or swapping out one unhealthy snack for a healthier option.

Starting with small changes also allows you to more easily integrate new habits into your daily life. Once you have successfully incorporated a new habit into your routine, you can gradually increase the time or effort you devote to it.

Beginning with small changes can help you establish a foundation for developing mindful habits and set you up for long-term success.

Set Realistic Goals: Identify specific, achievable goals that align with your values and priorities.

Setting realistic goals is an important strategy for cultivating mindful habits. When we set goals that are too lofty or unrealistic, we can quickly become discouraged and give up. On the other hand, setting goals that are too easy or don't align with our values and priorities may not provide enough motivation to sustain our efforts over the long term.

To set realistic goals—it's important to start by identifying what matters most to us. What values do we hold dear? What brings us a sense of purpose and meaning in our lives? Once we have a clear sense of our values and priorities, we can start to set goals that are in line with them.

When setting goals, it's important to make them specific and measurable. For example, instead of setting a vague goal like "I want to exercise more," we might set a specific goal like "I want to go for a 30-minute walk every day after work." This goal is specific, measurable, and achievable, which makes it more likely that we'll be able to stick with it over time.

It's also important to break larger goals down into smaller, more manageable steps. This can help us avoid feeling overwhelmed and make it easier to track our progress. For example, if our goal is to eat a healthier diet, we might start by adding one serving of vegetables to our meals each day and gradually increase from there.

By setting realistic goals that align with our values and priorities, we can cultivate mindful habits that support our overall well-being and enhance our quality of life.

Create a Routine: Establish a consistent routine that incorporates your mindful habits, making them easier to maintain over time.

Creating a routine is a powerful strategy for cultivating mindful habits. When you establish a consistent routine that includes your mindful habits, you make them a natural part of your day-to-day life, making it easier to maintain them over time.

To create a routine, start by identifying the mindful habits that you want to cultivate. Next, think about when and where you can incorporate these habits into your daily routine. For example, if you want to start a daily meditation practice, you might decide to meditate first thing in the morning before you begin your day.

Once you've identified when and where you'll practice your mindful habits, create a schedule or plan to ensure that you stick to your routine. Write down your schedule or use a calendar or app to keep track of your daily habits.

Remember to be flexible and adjust your routine as needed. Life can be unpredictable, and you may need to make changes to your routine to accommodate unexpected events or new priorities. But by establishing a consistent routine for your mindful habits, you'll make it easier to maintain these habits over time and experience the benefits of a more mindful life.

Practice Self-awareness: Observe your habits and notice how they affect your well-being, making adjustments as necessary.

Practising self-awareness is a critical strategy for cultivating mindful habits. Self-awareness involves paying attention to your thoughts, feelings, and behaviours without judgment. When you are aware of your habits, you can identify patterns that may be detrimental to your well-being and take steps to change them.

One way to practice self-awareness is to keep a journal or log of your habits. Write down what you do and when you do it, as well as any thoughts or emotions that arise before, during, or after the behaviour. This can help you identify triggers or patterns that may be contributing to unhealthy habits.

Another way to practice self-awareness is to use mindfulness techniques, such as meditation or breathing exercises, to become more present in the moment. When you are mindful, you can observe your thoughts and feelings without becoming attached to them, which can help you identify and change unhelpful patterns of behaviour.

Practising self-awareness can help you make conscious choices about your habits and empower you to make positive changes to your routine.

Be Accountable: Find an accountability partner or join a community to hold yourself accountable and receive support.

Accountability is an essential element in cultivating and maintaining mindful habits. It can be difficult to stay motivated and committed to new habits, especially if we try to go it alone. Having an accountability partner or being part of a community that shares our goals can provide the necessary support and encouragement to keep us on track.

An accountability partner is someone who shares our goals and is committed to helping us achieve them. This person can be a friend, family member, or colleague who we trust to hold us accountable and provide honest feedback. We can share our progress, challenges, and successes with them, and they can offer support, motivation, and accountability in return. The key is to choose someone who is reliable, supportive, and committed to our success.

Alternatively, we can join a community of like-minded individuals who share our goals and values. This can be a local group or an online community, and it can provide a sense of belonging, accountability, and support. Being part of a community can also offer opportunities for learning, growth, and connection with others who are on a similar journey.

By being accountable to ourselves and others, we can increase our motivation, overcome obstacles, and maintain our commitment to cultivating mindful habits. We can celebrate our successes and learn from our failures, and ultimately, we can create a more mindful, fulfilling, and intentional life.

Practice Self-compassion: Be kind to yourself and celebrate small wins, avoiding self-criticism and negative self-talk.

When it comes to cultivating mindful habits, it's important to practice self-compassion. This means being kind and understanding with yourself rather than being overly critical or judgmental. Self-compassion can help you stay motivated and committed to your mindful habits, even when things don't go as exactly planned.

One way to practice self-compassion is to celebrate your small wins. Recognize the progress you've made, even if it's just a small step in the right direction. For example, if you've been trying to develop a habit of daily meditation, celebrate the fact that you've meditated for five minutes every day for the past week rather than focusing on the fact that you haven't reached your goal of meditating for 20 minutes every day.

Another way to practice self-compassion is to avoid negative self-talk. Instead of criticizing yourself for not doing enough or not doing it perfectly, focus on the positive steps you've taken and give yourself credit for making an effort. Treat yourself with the same kindness and compassion you would offer a close friend who was struggling with a similar challenge.

It's important to remember that cultivating mindful habits is a process and that setbacks and challenges are a normal part of that process.

Be patient with yourself and try to approach your journey with curiosity and openness. With self-compassion, you can cultivate mindful habits that will help you live a more fulfilling and meaningful life.

Experiment: Try new habits and techniques to discover what works best for you

Experimentation is a crucial strategy for cultivating mindful habits. Trying new habits and techniques helps you to identify what works for you and what doesn't. This experimentation allows you to find new ways to incorporate mindfulness into your daily routine and make it more sustainable over time.

One approach to experimentation is to start with a small change, as mentioned earlier. For example, you could try adding five minutes of meditation to your morning routine. See how it feels and whether it's something you want to continue. If it works well, you can gradually increase the time or try a different mindfulness technique.

Another approach is to try different habits or techniques for a set period, such as a week or a month. For instance, you could try journaling every day for a month or going for a mindful walk each morning for a week. Take note of how you feel and whether the habit is having a positive impact on your well-being. If it's not working for you, don't be afraid to let it go and try something else.

Experimentation also involves being open to new ideas and being willing to learn from others. This can involve attending workshops or classes, reading books, or seeking guidance from a mindfulness teacher or coach. By being open to new perspectives and approaches, you can continue to grow and develop your mindful habits over time.

SECTION 3: EXAMPLES OF MINDFUL HABITS TO INCORPORATE INTO YOUR DAILY ROUTINE

Mindful Breathing Exercises: Take a few minutes each day to focus on your breath, calming your mind and reducing stress.

Mindful breathing exercises are a simple yet effective habit to incorporate into your daily routine. Taking a few minutes each day to focus on your breath can help calm your mind and reduce stress. This practice involves focusing your attention on the sensations of your breathing, such as the rise and fall of your chest or the feeling of air moving in and out of your nostrils. When your mind wanders, gently bring your attention back to your breath.

There are many different types of mindful breathing exercises to try. One common technique is diaphragmatic breathing, also known as belly breathing. This involves taking deep breaths from your diaphragm rather than shallow breaths from your chest. To do this, place one hand on your belly and the other on your chest. Take a slow, deep breath through your nose, feeling your belly rise as you inhale.

Exhale slowly through your mouth, feeling your belly fall as you exhale.

Another breathing exercise is called the 4-7-8 technique. To do this, inhale for four seconds, hold your breath for seven seconds, and exhale for eight seconds. Repeat this cycle several times, focusing on your breath and relaxing your body with each exhale.

Incorporating mindful breathing exercises into your daily routine can help improve your overall well-being by reducing stress and promoting relaxation. It can also improve your ability to focus and be present in the moment. Try incorporating this habit into your morning or evening routine or taking a few moments throughout the day to focus on your breath.

Gratitude Practice: Spend a few minutes each day reflecting on the things you are grateful for, increasing your overall sense of well-being and positivity.

Gratitude practice is a mindful habit that involves focusing on the positive things in your life and cultivating feelings of gratitude. By intentionally focusing on what you have rather than what you lack, you can increase your overall sense of well-being and positivity.

One way to incorporate gratitude practice into your daily routine is to set aside a few minutes each day to reflect on the things you are grateful for. This could be done in the morning as a way to start your day with a positive mindset or in the evening as a way to reflect on the events of the day and end on a positive note.

To practice gratitude, start by making a list of things you are grateful for. This could include things like your health, your family, your friends, your job, or even small moments of joy throughout your day. As you make your list, take the time to really savour and appreciate each item.

Another way to practice gratitude is to write a gratitude journal.

Each day, write down three to five things you are grateful for. This helps to cultivate a habit of noticing the positive things in your life and can be a helpful tool for reframing negative experiences.

Finally, you can practice gratitude by expressing it to others. Take the time to thank someone for something they have done for you or simply express your appreciation for their presence in your life. This not only cultivates gratitude within yourself but also strengthens your relationships with others.

Exercise: Incorporate movement into your daily routine, whether it's going for a walk, practising yoga, or hitting the gym

Regular physical exercise can help improve our physical and mental health, reducing stress and anxiety while boosting our mood and energy levels. When we exercise mindfully, we can further enhance these benefits by paying attention to our body and breathing and being present in the moment.

Some ways to incorporate exercise mindfully into our daily routine include:

1. **Walking meditation:** Take a mindful walk outdoors, paying attention to the sensation of your feet touching the ground, the sights and sounds around you, and your breath.
2. **Yoga:** Mindfully practising yoga can help improve our flexibility, strength, and balance while also promoting relaxation and stress reduction. Focus on your breath and body sensations during each pose, and allow yourself to be present in the moment.
3. **Strength training:** Lifting weights or doing other forms of strength training can be a great way to build physical strength and endurance while also promoting mental focus and resilience. Pay attention to your form and breathing, and allow yourself to feel present and focused on each movement.

4. **Mindful cardio:** Whether you prefer running, cycling, or swimming, incorporating cardio exercise into your routine can help improve cardiovascular health, reduce stress, and increase endurance. Focus on your breath and body sensations during each movement and allow yourself to feel present and focused in the moment.

Mindful Eating: Pay attention to your body's hunger and fullness cues, savouring each bite and practising mindful portion control.

Mindful eating is a habit that involves paying close attention to the food you are consuming and the experience of eating it. This habit can help to increase your awareness of your body's hunger and fullness signals, which can, in turn, help you to eat in a way that is more balanced and satisfying. When practising mindful eating, you should take the time to savour each bite of your food, paying attention to the flavours, textures, and aromas. You can also pay attention to the way your body responds to the food, noting any sensations or feelings that arise.

In addition, practising mindful eating can help you to practice portion control as you become more aware of the amount of food that you are consuming. By tuning in to your body's signals of fullness, you can learn to stop eating when you are satisfied rather than continuing to eat out of habit or boredom.

To incorporate mindful eating into your daily routine, try turning off any distractions, such as the TV or phone, while you eat, and focus solely on the experience of eating. Take the time to prepare your food mindfully and choose foods that are nourishing and satisfying. You may also find it helpful to practice gratitude before your meals, acknowledging the effort that went into growing, preparing, and providing your food.

Digital Detox: Take a break from technology, reduce distractions, and increase focus.

Digital detox is a mindful habit that involves intentionally disconnecting from technology and taking a break from screens. In today's digital age, it's easy to become overstimulated and overwhelmed by the constant barrage of notifications, emails, and social media updates. This can lead to feelings of stress, anxiety, and burnout.

By incorporating a digital detox into your daily routine, you can reduce these negative effects and improve your overall well-being. Some strategies for a digital detox include:

1. **Establish boundaries:** Set designated times each day when you will check your phone or computer and stick to those times. This will help you avoid the temptation to constantly check for new notifications.
2. **Take breaks**: Throughout the day, take short breaks from screens. Go for a walk, do some stretching, or engage in another activity that doesn't involve technology.
3. **Turn off notifications**: Disable unnecessary notifications on your phone and computer to reduce distractions.
4. **Create tech-free zones**: Designate certain areas of your home or workspace as technology-free zones, such as the bedroom or dining room.
5. **Practice mindfulness:** Use the time you would normally spend on your phone or computer to practice mindfulness meditation, journaling, or other mindfulness activities.

Incorporating a digital detox into your daily routine can help you feel more present, focused, and relaxed. It can also improve your sleep, reduce stress levels, and increase your overall well-being.

Journaling: Spend a few minutes each day reflecting on your thoughts and emotions, increasing self-awareness and promoting personal growth

Journaling is a powerful way to incorporate mindfulness into your daily routine. By writing down your thoughts and feelings, you can gain insight into your inner world and develop a greater sense of self-awareness. Journaling can also help you process difficult emotions, reduce stress, and promote personal growth.

To start journaling practice, set aside a few minutes each day to write down your thoughts and feelings. You can use a physical notebook or a digital platform, whichever feels most comfortable for you. Try to write without judgment or self-criticism, simply allowing your thoughts to flow onto the page.

You might start by reflecting on your day or on a specific event or experience that has been on your mind. Consider how you felt during the experience and what thoughts and emotions came up for you. You might also write about your goals, aspirations, and values or explore your personal relationships and how they impact your well-being.

Remember that journaling is a personal practice, and there is no right or wrong way to do it. The goal is simply to become more aware of your thoughts and emotions and to develop greater self-understanding and compassion. Over time, you may find that journaling becomes a valuable tool for managing stress, reducing anxiety, and promoting overall well-being.

Mindful Communication: Practice active listening, empathy, and non-judgmental communication to improve your relationships and overall well-being.

Mindful communication is the practice of being present and fully engaged in the communication process, with an emphasis on listening and understanding. It involves paying attention to the words, tone, and body language of the person you are communicating with, as well as your own responses and reactions. Here are some tips for incorporating mindful communication into your daily routine:

1. **Practice active listening:** When someone is speaking to you, give them your full attention. Focus on what they are saying rather than thinking about what you will say next.
2. **Use empathy**: Put yourself in the other person's shoes and try to see the situation from their perspective. This will help you to better understand their point of view.
3. **Avoid judgment**: Try to suspend judgment and avoid jumping to conclusions. Instead, focus on understanding the other person's perspective.
4. **Practice non-judgmental communication**: Avoid using judgmental language and instead use neutral language that is focused on describing what you are experiencing or feeling.
5. **Be present:** Stay present in the conversation and avoid distractions. Put away your phone and other devices to ensure that you are fully engaged in the conversation.

Incorporating mindful communication into your daily routine can improve your relationships and overall well-being. It can also help you to communicate more effectively and resolve conflicts in a more positive and constructive manner.

Adding mindful habits into your daily routine can have a significant impact on your well-being and overall quality of life. By prioritizing self-awareness, self-care, and personal growth, you can cultivate habits that align with your goals and values, leading to increased focus, productivity, and happiness.

Remember to start small, be kind to yourself, and experiment with different techniques to discover what works best for you. With time and consistency, these mindful habits can become an integral part of your daily routine, helping you to live a more fulfilling and meaningful life.

THE ROLE OF HABITS IN PRODUCTIVITY AND WELL-BEING

Habits play a crucial role in both productivity and well-being. Our daily habits, whether good or bad, shape our behaviours and ultimately determine our outcomes in life. By incorporating mindful habits into our daily routines, we can enhance our productivity and well-being.

Productivity is directly linked to our habits. When we have good habits, we are more efficient and effective in our work. On the other hand, when we have bad habits, we can become easily distracted, procrastinate, and waste time. Mindful habits can help us overcome these challenges and improve our productivity.

One way that mindful habits improve productivity is by reducing decision fatigue. When we have established habits, we don't have to waste mental energy making decisions about what to do next. For example, suppose we habitually exercise first thing in the morning. In that case, we don't have to spend time deciding whether to exercise or not. We just do it automatically, freeing up mental energy for other tasks.

In addition, mindful habits can help us stay focused and avoid distractions. For example, suppose we have a habit of setting aside a specific time each day to check our email. In that case, we can avoid getting distracted by incoming messages throughout the day. This helps us stay focused on our priorities and ultimately get more done.

Furthermore, mindful habits can also improve our well-being. Good habits—such as regular exercise, healthy eating, and getting enough sleep have been shown to improve physical health, mental health, and overall well-being. By incorporating these habits into our daily routines, we can reduce stress, increase energy, and improve our mood.

In contrast, bad habits, such as excessive screen time, poor diet, and lack of exercise, can negatively impact our well-being. By replacing these bad habits with mindful habits, we can improve our physical and mental health, leading to a better quality of life.

The role of habits in productivity and well-being cannot be overstated. By incorporating mindful habits into our daily routines, we can improve productivity, reduce stress, and enhance our overall well-being.

HOW TO CREATE AND MAINTAIN PRODUCTIVE HABITS

Creating and maintaining productive habits can be challenging, but it is an essential part of achieving your goals and improving your overall well-being. Here are some steps to help you create and maintain productive habits:

1. **Identify your goals:** Before you can create productive habits, you need to identify what you want to achieve. Write down your short-term and long-term goals, and be specific about what you want to accomplish.
2. **Choose the habits:** Once you have identified your goals, choose the habits that will help you achieve them. For example, if your goal is to improve your fitness, your habits might include working out for 30 minutes each day or going for a walk after dinner.
3. **Start small:** Don't try to change all your habits at once. Start with one or two small habits and gradually build up over time. This will help you avoid overwhelming and make it easier to maintain your habits.
4. **Create a routine:** Incorporate your new habits into your daily routine, making them a part of your daily life. For example, if your new habit is to meditate for 10 minutes each morning, make it a part of your morning routine.
5. **Track your progress:** Keep track of your progress and celebrate small wins along the way. This will help you stay motivated and on track.
6. **Be accountable:** Find an accountability partner or join a

community to hold yourself accountable and receive support. This can help you stay motivated and make it easier to maintain your habits.

7. **Practice self-compassion:** Be kind to yourself and avoid self-criticism. If you slip up, don't beat yourself up. Instead, focus on getting back on track and continuing to make progress.
8. **Stay flexible:** Remember that life is unpredictable, and sometimes things don't go according to plan. Be willing to adjust your habits and routine as needed to accommodate changes in your life.

By following these steps, you can create and maintain productive habits that will help you achieve your goals and improve your overall well-being. Remember to be patient with yourself and celebrate your progress along the way.

TIPS FOR BREAKING UNPRODUCTIVE HABITS AND REPLACING THEM WITH BETTER

Breaking unproductive habits can be challenging, but with mindful awareness and deliberate effort, it is possible to replace them with better, more productive habits. Here are some tips for breaking unproductive habits and creating new, healthier ones:

1. **Identify the unproductive habit:** The first step to breaking an unproductive habit is to identify it. This requires honest self-reflection and awareness of your behaviours.
2. **Understand the trigger:** Once you have identified the unproductive habit, it's important to understand what triggers it. This could be a specific situation, emotion, or environment that prompts the habit.
3. **Create a plan:** Develop a plan for how you will replace the unproductive habit with a better one. Identify the new habit you want to create and create an action plan for how you will implement it.
4. **Use positive reinforcement:** Positive reinforcement can help you stick to your new habit. Reward yourself for making progress and achieving milestones along the way.
5. **Practice self-compassion:** Breaking an unproductive habit can be challenging, so it's important to practice self-compassion. Be patient with yourself and acknowledge that change takes time.
6. **Seek support:** Surround yourself with people who support your new habit and can hold you accountable. Joining a group or finding an accountability partner can also be helpful.

7. **Practice mindfulness:** Mindfulness can help you become more aware of your thoughts and behaviours, making it easier to identify unproductive habits and replace them with better ones.

Remember, breaking unproductive habits takes time and effort, but it's worth it in the long run. By replacing unproductive habits with better ones, you can improve your productivity, well-being, and overall quality of life.

CHAPTER 8

MINDFUL LEADERSHIP

In today's fast-paced business environment, leaders are under increasing pressure to deliver results, often at the expense of their own well-being and that of their teams. Mindful leadership offers a new approach, emphasizing the importance of awareness, empathy, and ethical decision-making to drive performance and foster a positive work environment.

Incorporating mindfulness into leadership practices has numerous benefits. First and foremost, it can lead to improved well-being, reducing stress and increasing resilience in leaders and their teams. Mindfulness also improves cognitive functioning, including attention, memory, and decision-making, leading to better problem-solving and strategic planning. Furthermore, mindfulness has been shown to increase emotional intelligence, improving communication and relationships within teams and with external stakeholders.

In addition to these personal benefits, implementing mindful leadership principles can have a positive impact on organizational culture. Leaders who model mindfulness behaviours can inspire their teams to be more engaged and productive, leading to better business outcomes. Furthermore, a culture of mindfulness can foster creativity and innovation, as team members feel more empowered to take risks and share ideas.

To develop mindful leadership skills, leaders can start by practising mindfulness themselves, incorporating meditation, breathing exercises, and other techniques into their daily routines. They can also work on developing empathy and emotional intelligence by actively listening to and engaging with team members and practising non-judgmental communication. Finally, leaders can model ethical behaviour by making decisions based on principles such as fairness, honesty, and respect.

Incorporating mindfulness into leadership practices offers numerous benefits, including improved well-being, cognitive functioning, emotional intelligence, and organizational culture. By developing mindful leadership skills, leaders can improve team performance, increase employee engagement and retention, and foster a positive work environment, ultimately leading to better business outcomes.

THE CONCEPT OF MINDFULNESS AND ITS APPLICATION IN LEADERSHIP

The concept of mindfulness has gained increasing popularity in recent years and for good reason. Mindfulness is a state of being fully present and engaged in the current moment without judgment or distraction. It involves paying attention to thoughts, emotions, and physical sensations and accepting them without trying to change or suppress them.

In leadership, mindfulness can be a valuable tool for enhancing self-awareness, emotional intelligence, and decision-making. Mindful leaders are better able to manage stress, communicate effectively, and build strong relationships with their teams. They are more attuned to their own needs and the needs of others and can respond to challenges with greater clarity and compassion.

Furthermore, mindful leadership emphasizes the importance of values-driven decision-making, ethical conduct, and social responsibility. By cultivating mindfulness in leadership, individuals can create more sustainable and socially responsible organizations that prioritize the well-being of all stakeholders.

The application of mindfulness in leadership can lead to greater personal and professional growth, improved team dynamics, and a more positive impact on society.

THE IMPORTANCE OF ETHICAL AND COMPASSIONATE LEADERSHIP, WHICH ALIGNS WITH THE PRINCIPLES OF MINDFULNESS.

Ethical and compassionate leadership is crucial in any organization or community, and it aligns perfectly with the principles of mindfulness. Mindfulness is not just about being present and aware; it is also about being ethical and compassionate in our actions and decisions. Ethical leadership involves making decisions based on values and principles that prioritize the well-being of all stakeholders, including employees, customers, and the wider community.

Compassionate leadership, on the other hand, involves showing empathy and kindness towards others, understanding their needs and concerns, and treating them with respect and dignity. This type of leadership fosters a positive work environment and promotes well-being and productivity among team members.

When leaders practice mindfulness, they are better equipped to make ethical and compassionate decisions. By being present and fully engaged, they can consider all the perspectives and implications of their decisions and make choices that align with their values and principles. Mindful leaders are also better able to regulate their emotions and respond to challenges in a calm and compassionate manner, which helps to foster a positive and supportive work environment.

In addition, ethical and compassionate leadership is essential for building trust and fostering positive relationships with stakeholders. When leaders prioritize the well-being of others and act with integrity and compassion, they earn the respect and loyalty of their team members, customers, and community. This, in turn, can lead to increased engagement, productivity, and profitability for the organization.

Ethical and compassionate leadership is a critical component of mindful leadership. By incorporating these principles into their leadership style, leaders can create a positive and supportive work environment, build trust and loyalty, and make decisions that align with their values and principles.

How can mindful leadership improve team performance, increase employee engagement and retention, and foster a positive work environment?

Mindful leadership can have a significant positive impact on team performance, employee engagement and retention, and the overall work environment. Here are some ways in which mindful leadership can contribute to these outcomes:

1. **Improved communication**: Mindful leaders are more attentive and present during conversations, which can lead to clearer communication and better understanding among team members. This can help reduce misunderstandings and conflicts, leading to a more positive work environment.
2. **Better decision-making**: Mindful leaders are more aware of their thoughts and emotions, which can help them make better decisions. They are also more open to feedback and perspectives from others, which can lead to more well-

rounded decisions that take into account the needs and perspectives of everyone involved.

3. **Increased engagement and motivation:** Mindful leaders create an environment that values and promotes well-being, which can lead to increased engagement and motivation among team members. When employees feel that their well-being is a priority, they are more likely to be committed to their work and the organization.
4. **Enhanced creativity:** Mindful leaders encourage creativity by creating a space for reflection and exploration. This can lead to the development of new ideas and innovative solutions to problems.
5. **Improved resilience:** Mindful leaders create an environment that supports and encourages self-care and resilience. This can help employees cope with stress and challenges more effectively, leading to increased productivity and reduced burnout.

Mindful leadership can contribute to a positive and productive work environment where employees feel valued, engaged, and supported. This can lead to improved team performance, increased employee retention, and a stronger organizational culture.

HOW MINDFUL LEADERS CAN INSPIRE CREATIVITY AND INNOVATION IN THEIR TEAMS.

Mindful leaders can inspire creativity and innovation in their teams by creating a work environment that supports and encourages these qualities. When leaders practice mindfulness, they are able to cultivate a non-judgmental and open-minded approach, which allows their team members to feel safe and supported in expressing their ideas.

Mindful leaders also foster a culture of curiosity and learning, which encourages their team members to explore new ideas and approaches. By emphasizing the importance of experimentation and taking calculated risks, mindful leaders can help their teams to generate new and innovative ideas.

In addition, mindful leaders recognize the importance of self-care and stress reduction in promoting creativity and innovation. By encouraging their team members to take breaks, practice mindfulness, and engage in other stress-reducing activities, leaders can help to reduce burnout and promote a more balanced and productive work environment.

Mindful leaders who prioritize creativity and innovation can help their teams to stay ahead of the curve in their industry and to develop innovative solutions that can drive business growth and success.

THE IMPORTANCE OF IMPLEMENTING MINDFUL LEADERSHIP PRINCIPLES IN ORGANIZATIONAL CULTURE

Implementing mindful leadership principles in organizational culture can have a significant impact on the overall success of the organization. When leaders prioritize mindfulness and incorporate it into the culture, employees are more likely to feel valued, supported, and motivated to contribute their best work.

Mindful leadership principles, such as active listening, empathy, and non-judgmental communication, can help create an environment where employees feel heard, understood, and respected. When leaders prioritize these principles, employees are more likely to feel safe to express their ideas and opinions, leading to increased collaboration and creativity.

In addition, implementing mindful leadership principles can help improve employee well-being and reduce stress levels. Mindful leaders prioritize work-life balance and encourage employees to take breaks and prioritize self-care. This can lead to increased employee engagement and retention, as well as improved mental health and overall job satisfaction.

Incorporation of mindful leadership principles into organizational culture can lead to a more positive and productive work environment, with higher levels of employee engagement, creativity, and well-being.

HOW TO APPLY MINDFUL PRODUCTIVITY PRINCIPLES TO LEADERSHIP ROLES

Mindful productivity principles can be applied to leadership roles in various ways to improve performance, increase employee engagement and retention, and foster a positive work environment. Here are some practical strategies for incorporating mindful productivity principles into leadership practices:

1. **Practice self-awareness**: Mindful leaders must first be aware of their own emotions and behaviours. By practising self-awareness, leaders can better understand their own strengths and weaknesses, as well as their impact on others. This can help them develop more effective communication and leadership strategies.
2. **Foster a positive work environment:** Mindful leaders create a positive work environment by modelling the behaviour they expect from their employees. This means being respectful, empathetic, and compassionate towards others, as well as encouraging and acknowledging their contributions. By creating a positive work environment, leaders can improve employee engagement and retention.
3. **Encourage mindfulness practices:** Mindful leaders can encourage mindfulness practices such as meditation, breathing exercises, and yoga to help employees reduce stress, increase focus, and improve overall well-being. This can also help create a culture of mindfulness within the organization.
4. **Prioritize employee well-being**: Mindful leaders prioritize employee well-being by encouraging work-life balance, providing opportunities for growth and development, and

ensuring fair and equitable treatment. This can improve employee morale and lead to increased productivity and performance.

5. **Practice effective communication:** Mindful leaders practice effective communication by actively listening, providing feedback, and being transparent and honest in their communication. This can help build trust and strengthen relationships with employees.
6. **Foster creativity and innovation:** Mindful leaders foster creativity and innovation by encouraging open communication, providing opportunities for experimentation, and recognizing and rewarding new ideas. This can lead to increased innovation and improved business outcomes.

By incorporating mindful productivity principles into their leadership practices, leaders can create a more positive and productive work environment, improve employee engagement and retention, and drive better business outcomes.

STRATEGIES FOR LEADING WITH EMPATHY AND COMPASSION

Leading with empathy and compassion is an essential aspect of mindful leadership. Empathy involves understanding and sharing the feelings of others, while compassion involves taking action to alleviate their suffering. When leaders lead with empathy and compassion, they can create a supportive and caring environment that fosters engagement, creativity, and productivity. Here are some strategies for incorporating empathy and compassion into leadership practices:

1. **Active listening:** Leaders should listen actively and attentively to their team members. This means putting aside distractions and truly focusing on what the other person is saying. Active listening involves asking questions, clarifying, and summarizing to ensure that you understand what the other person is saying.
2. **Acknowledge emotions**: Emotions are a natural part of the human experience, and it is essential to acknowledge them. When team members feel heard and understood, they are more likely to be engaged and committed to their work.
3. **Offer support:** Leaders should offer support to team members in times of need. This could be anything from providing resources to helping with workload management.
4. **Practice gratitude:** Gratitude involves recognizing and appreciating the contributions of others. Leaders should regularly express gratitude to their team members and acknowledge their hard work and accomplishments.
5. **Encourage self-care**: Leaders should encourage team members to prioritize self-care and take time to recharge.

This could involve offering flexible work arrangements or promoting wellness initiatives.

6. **Lead by example**: Leaders should lead by example and model empathy and compassion in their own behaviour. This means being transparent, authentic, and vulnerable when appropriate and demonstrating a commitment to the well-being of team members.

By incorporating these strategies into leadership practices, leaders can create a culture of empathy and compassion that supports the well-being and productivity of their team members.

THE BENEFITS OF EMPOWERING AND SUPPORTING YOUR TEAM MEMBERS

As a mindful leader, one of the key goals is to empower and support team members. Empowering team members involves giving them the necessary tools, resources, and support to succeed in their roles. This can include providing ongoing training and development opportunities, allowing them to take ownership of their work, and encouraging them to take risks and make decisions.

When team members feel empowered, they are more likely to take the initiative, innovate, and contribute to the organization's success. Empowered employees also tend to be more engaged and committed to their work, which can lead to higher productivity and job satisfaction.

Supporting team members involves providing emotional and practical support. This can include listening to their concerns, providing feedback and coaching, and offering resources to help them manage stress and workload. When leaders provide this type of support, it can create a positive work environment and improve overall team morale.

In addition to these benefits, empowering and supporting team members can also lead to increased trust and respect between leaders and their teams. This, in turn, can create a culture of collaboration, innovation, and high performance.

Strategies for empowering and supporting team members include:

- **Providing regular feedback and recognition**

Providing regular feedback and recognition is an essential component of empowering and supporting team members. Mindful leaders understand the importance of acknowledging their team members' efforts and contributions regularly. By doing so, they can boost their team's morale, motivation, and engagement levels.

Regular feedback can take various forms, including constructive criticism, positive reinforcement, and coaching. Constructive criticism should always be delivered in a respectful and non-judgmental manner, focusing on specific behaviours rather than personal traits. Positive reinforcement can come in the form of verbal or written recognition, highlighting a team member's achievements or efforts. Coaching involves providing guidance and support to help team members improve their skills and achieve their goals.

For instance, a mindful leader might provide regular feedback and recognition to their team members by scheduling weekly check-ins. During these meetings, the leader might ask team members about their progress, offer feedback on their performance, and provide recognition for their achievements. The leader might also ask team members for feedback, encouraging open and honest communication. Additionally, the leader might provide coaching and support to help team members develop their skills and achieve their goals.

Another example of providing regular feedback and recognition is through team-wide communication channels. A mindful leader might use company-wide emails or meetings to recognize team members' achievements and share feedback. For example, they might send an email to the team congratulating a team member who has gone above and beyond their duties, highlighting their specific achievements, and expressing gratitude for their hard work.

Regular feedback and recognition are crucial components of mindful leadership. By providing constructive criticism, positive reinforcement, and coaching, leaders can empower their team members, boost their motivation, and create a positive work environment.

- **Encouraging open communication and collaboration**

Encouraging open communication and collaboration is a key aspect of leading with empathy and compassion. Mindful leaders recognize that their team members are unique individuals with different strengths, perspectives, and ideas, and they value and respect these differences. They also understand that fostering a culture of open communication and collaboration can lead to increased productivity, better decision-making, and higher job satisfaction among team members.

To encourage open communication and collaboration, mindful leaders can implement various strategies. For example, they can hold regular team meetings where everyone has the opportunity to share their thoughts and ideas. They can also create channels for ongoing feedback and suggestions, such as an anonymous suggestion box or regular one-on-one meetings with team members.

Another way to encourage collaboration is by creating opportunities for team members to work together on projects or assignments. This can include assigning group projects, cross-training team members on different skills, or holding team-building activities such as group brainstorming sessions or team-building exercises.

Mindful leaders also recognize the importance of active listening and empathy when it comes to communication and collaboration. They make an effort to listen to their team members without judgment or interruption, and they seek to understand their perspectives and needs. They also make an effort to communicate clearly and effectively, using non-judgmental language and being open to feedback and suggestions.

For example, a mindful leader might encourage their team members to share their ideas openly by asking open-ended questions like "What do you think about this idea?" or "What would you do differently?" They might also make an effort to express their own thoughts and opinions in a clear and constructive way, using "I" statements instead of "you" statements and being open to feedback and suggestions from their team members.

Encouraging open communication and collaboration is an important strategy for mindful leaders who want to create a positive and productive work environment for their team members. By fostering an environment of trust, respect, and empathy, they can help their team members feel valued and supported, which can lead to increased engagement, motivation, and satisfaction in their work.

- **Creating a supportive and inclusive work environment**

Creating a supportive and inclusive work environment is essential for empowering and supporting team members. Mindful leaders recognize the importance of diversity, equity, and inclusion in the workplace and strive to create an environment where everyone feels welcome and valued.

One way to create a supportive and inclusive work environment is to provide equal opportunities for all team members. This means creating a workplace culture that values and respects the diverse backgrounds, experiences, and perspectives of all team members. Mindful leaders ensure that all team members have access to the same resources and opportunities for professional growth and development.

Another important aspect of creating a supportive and inclusive work environment is promoting work-life balance. Mindful leaders understand that their team members have lives outside of work and need to have the flexibility to attend to their personal and family responsibilities. This may include offering flexible work arrangements, such as remote work options or flexible schedules, to help team members manage their work and personal obligations.

Additionally, mindful leaders prioritize mental and physical well-being in the workplace. This may involve offering wellness programs or initiatives, such as on-site fitness classes or mental health resources, to support team members in maintaining their well-being.

Finally, creating a supportive and inclusive work environment also involves fostering a sense of belonging among team members. This can be achieved by promoting teamwork, collaboration, and open communication. Mindful leaders encourage team members to share their ideas and perspectives and work together to achieve common goals. By creating an environment where team members feel included and supported, mindful leaders can help to improve overall team performance and productivity.

- **Providing opportunities for professional growth and development**

Providing opportunities for professional growth and development is an important aspect of empowering and supporting team members. Mindful leaders recognize the value of investing in their employee's growth and development, both for the benefit of the individual and the organization as a whole. Some strategies for providing opportunities for professional growth and development include:

1. **Offering training and development programs:** Providing training and development programs, such as workshops, seminars, and online courses, can help team members build new skills and knowledge relevant to their roles. For example, a mindful leader may provide a training program on effective communication, time management, or leadership skills to help team members improve their performance.
2. **Encouraging learning and knowledge-sharing:** Mindful leaders encourage a culture of learning and knowledge-sharing by providing opportunities for team members to attend conferences, participate in webinars, or share their

expertise with others in the organization. For example, a leader may encourage team members to attend a conference on the latest industry trends and share their learnings with the team.

3. **Providing mentoring and coaching:** Providing mentorship and coaching opportunities to team members can be a valuable way to support their growth and development. A mindful leader may assign a mentor to a team member to provide guidance and feedback on specific skills or areas for improvement.
4. **Creating opportunities for career advancement:** Mindful leaders create pathways for team members to advance in their careers within the organization. This may involve setting goals and providing support to help team members achieve them, providing opportunities for leadership roles or project management, or advocating for promotions or new job opportunities within the organization.

By providing opportunities for professional growth and development, mindful leaders demonstrate their commitment to their team members' success and create a positive and supportive work environment that fosters productivity, engagement, and innovation.

- **Encouraging self-care and work-life balance**

Encouraging self-care and work-life balance is an important aspect of empowering and supporting team members in a mindful leadership approach. Mindful leaders recognize that their team members are not just employees but individuals with their own personal lives and responsibilities outside of work. Therefore, it's crucial to encourage self-care and work-life balance to avoid burnout and increase overall job satisfaction.

One way to encourage self-care is to offer resources and support for mental health, such as an Employee Assistance Program (EAP), which provides confidential counselling and support for employees facing personal and work-related issues. Mindful leaders can also encourage their team members to take breaks throughout the workday and to practice mindfulness and stress-management techniques, such as meditation or deep breathing exercises.

To promote work-life balance, mindful leaders can offer flexible work arrangements, such as remote work options or flexible scheduling. This can help employees manage personal responsibilities, such as caring for children or elderly parents, while still meeting their work responsibilities. Mindful leaders can also set an example by modelling healthy work-life boundaries, such as not sending work emails outside of normal work hours.

Encouraging self-care and work-life balance can lead to increased job satisfaction, productivity, and overall well-being for team members. It can also improve team morale and create a positive work environment where individuals feel valued and supported.

- **Leading by example and modelling positive behaviours**

Leading by example and modelling positive behaviours is an important aspect of mindful leadership. It involves setting an example for your team members by demonstrating positive behaviours and values, which can inspire and motivate them to do the same. Here are some examples of how leaders can lead by example:

1. **Time management:** Leaders can model good time management habits by being punctual, prioritizing tasks, and avoiding procrastination. This can set a positive tone for the team and encourage them to manage their time effectively.
2. **Work-life balance:** Leaders can encourage work-life balance by setting realistic expectations for workload, taking breaks,

and avoiding burnout. This can show team members that it is possible to balance work and personal life.

3. **Ethical behaviour:** Leaders can model ethical behaviour by being honest, transparent, and accountable. This can set a standard for the team and help to build trust and respect.
4. **Collaboration:** Leaders can model collaboration by working with team members and encouraging them to work together. This can foster a sense of teamwork and promote a positive work environment.
5. **Continuous learning:** Leaders can model continuous learning by seeking out opportunities for professional development, sharing their knowledge and skills, and encouraging team members to do the same. This can create a culture of learning and growth within the organization.

By leading by example and modelling positive behaviours, leaders can set the tone for the team and create a culture of mindfulness, positivity, and productivity.

Incorporating these strategies into leadership practices can create a positive and empowering work environment that benefits both the organization and its team members.

CHAPTER 9

MINDFUL PRODUCTIVITY IN PRACTICE

The chapter on "Mindful Productivity in Practice" is all about taking the concepts and principles discussed in the earlier parts of the book and applying them to your daily life. It's about putting theory into action and developing habits and practices that will help you become more mindful and productive in your work and personal life.

The chapter will provide practical strategies and exercises to help you incorporate mindfulness into your daily routine and enhance your productivity. The focus will be on developing habits that promote focus, creativity, and self-awareness while reducing stress and increasing overall well-being.

Some of the key topics that will be covered in this chapter include:

1. **Mindful time management:** Strategies for prioritizing tasks, avoiding distractions, and using your time more effectively.
2. **Mindful goal setting:** Techniques for setting goals that align with your values and priorities and developing action plans to achieve them.
3. **Mindful communication:** Tools for improving communication with others, including active listening and effective feedback.
4. **Mindful self-care:** Practices for taking care of your physical,

mental, and emotional health, including exercise, meditation, and healthy eating.

5. **Mindful reflection:** Strategies for reflecting on your progress, learning from your mistakes, and setting new intentions for the future.

Throughout the chapter, there will be exercises, prompts, and activities to help you put these concepts into practice and integrate them into your daily routine.

By the end of the chapter, you will have a better understanding of how to apply mindful productivity principles to your work and personal life, leading to increased focus, productivity, and overall well-being.

Mindful time management: Strategies for prioritizing tasks, avoiding distractions, and using your time more effectively.

Mindful time management is all about being intentional with your time and using it in a way that aligns with your priorities and values. It involves setting clear goals, prioritizing tasks, avoiding distractions, and focusing on one thing at a time. By practising mindful time management, you can increase your productivity, reduce stress, and achieve a greater sense of satisfaction and fulfilment in your work and personal life.

Exercises:

1. **Set SMART goals:** Take some time to reflect on what you want to achieve in the next week, month, or year. Write down your goals using the SMART framework: Specific, Measurable, Achievable, Relevant, and Time-bound. For example, instead of setting a vague goal like "exercise more,"

try setting a SMART goal like "go for a 30-minute walk three times a week for the next month."

2. **Prioritize your tasks:** Make a list of all the tasks you need to accomplish today or this week. Then, rank them in order of importance using the Eisenhower Matrix: Urgent and important, Important but not urgent, Urgent but not important, and neither urgent nor important. Focus on completing the tasks in the important and urgent quadrant first.
3. **Practice single-tasking:** Instead of trying to do multiple things at once, focus on one task at a time. Set a timer for 25 minutes and work on that task without any distractions. Then, take a five-minute break before starting the next task.

Prompts:

1. What are some of the biggest timewasters in your day? How can you eliminate or reduce them?
2. What are your top three priorities for the week? How can you make sure you allocate enough time and energy to each of them?
3. When do you feel most productive and focused? How can you schedule your tasks to align with your natural rhythms?

Activities:

1. **Create a daily or weekly schedule:** Use a planner or digital tool to block off time for your most important tasks, as well as time for breaks and self-care activities. Stick to your schedule as much as possible to develop a routine and avoid overcommitting yourself.
2. **Use a time tracker:** Keep track of how you spend your time

for a day or a week using a time tracking tool or a simple spreadsheet. Review your results to identify patterns and areas where you can make adjustments.

3. **Practice mindfulness meditation:** Set aside 10-15 minutes each day to practice mindfulness meditation. Focus on your breath and observe any thoughts or emotions that arise without judgment. This can help you develop a greater sense of self-awareness and reduce stress and anxiety.

Mindful goal setting: Techniques for setting goals that align with your values and priorities and developing action plans to achieve them.

Mindful goal setting involves setting goals that are meaningful and aligned with your values and priorities. It also involves developing action plans that are achievable, realistic, and adaptable. By setting mindful goals and developing action plans, you can increase your motivation, focus, and productivity and reduce your stress and overwhelm. Here are some techniques for setting mindful goals and developing action plans:

Exercises:

1. **Values clarification exercise:** Write down your top five values (e.g., honesty, compassion, creativity, freedom, health). Then, rank them in order of importance. Next, think about how you can align your goals with your values. For example, if creativity is one of your top values, you might set a goal to write a novel, paint a portrait, or learn a new instrument.
2. **SMART goal-setting exercise:** Use the SMART criteria to set a goal that is Specific, Measurable, Achievable, Realistic, and Time-bound. For example, instead of setting a vague goal like "exercise more," set a SMART goal like "run for 30 minutes

three times a week for the next month."

Prompts:

1. What are your top three priorities in life? How can you set goals that align with these priorities?
2. What are some goals you have set in the past that were not aligned with your values or priorities? How did you feel about these goals? What can you do differently next time?

Activities:

1. **Mindful goal-setting worksheet:** Use a worksheet to clarify your values, set SMART goals, and develop action plans. Include sections for brainstorming, prioritizing, and scheduling.
2. **Visualization exercise:** Visualize yourself achieving your goals. Use all your senses to imagine what it will look, feel, sound, smell, and taste like when you achieve your goals. Write down your visualization and read it aloud to yourself regularly to stay motivated and focused.
3. **Goal reflection exercise:** Set aside some time each week to reflect on your progress toward your goals. Ask yourself what went well, what could have gone better, and what adjustments you need to make going forward. Write down your reflections and use them to adjust your action plans as needed.

These exercises, prompts, and activities can help you set mindful goals and develop action plans that align with your values and priorities. By practising mindful goal setting, you can increase your productivity, motivation, and well-being.

Mindful communication: Tools for improving communication with others, including active listening and effective feedback.

Effective communication is essential for success in both personal and professional life. Mindful communication involves active listening, empathy, and non-judgmental communication, which can help to build stronger relationships, resolve conflicts, and foster a more positive and supportive work environment. In this chapter, we will explore some tools and techniques for improving communication with others and enhancing the quality of our relationships.

Exercises:

1. **Mindful Listening:** Choose a partner and take turns sharing a story or experience with each other. While one person is sharing, the other person should focus on actively listening without interrupting or judging. After the speaker has finished, the listener should summarize what they heard and ask clarifying questions. Then switch roles and repeat the exercise.
2. **Non-Judgmental Communication:** Practice expressing your thoughts and feelings without judgment or criticism. Start by choosing a neutral topic and share your thoughts and feelings about it with someone. Pay attention to any judgments or criticisms that come up, and try to rephrase your thoughts and feelings without them. For example, instead of saying, "I hate this weather," you could say, "I find it challenging to deal with this weather."

Prompts:

1. What are some common communication barriers that can hinder effective communication?
2. What are some ways to express empathy and understanding

in communication?

3. How can non-judgmental communication improve relationships?

Activities:

1. **Role-Playing:** Create a role-playing scenario in which you practice mindful communication in a challenging situation. For example, you could practice communicating with a difficult coworker or having a challenging conversation with a family member.
2. **Feedback Practice:** Practice giving and receiving feedback with a partner. Choose a topic to provide feedback on, such as a recent project or presentation. Practice giving feedback that is specific, non-judgmental, and focused on behaviour. Then switch roles and repeat the exercise.

These exercises, prompts, and activities can help to improve your communication skills and enhance your relationships with others, leading to greater success and fulfilment in your personal and professional life.

Mindful self-care: Practices for taking care of your physical, mental, and emotional health, including exercise, meditation, and healthy eating.

Taking care of yourself is crucial for maintaining productivity and overall well-being. Mindful self-care practices can help you manage stress, increase focus and concentration, and boost your mood. In this chapter, we will explore some effective strategies for taking care of your physical, mental, and emotional health.

Exercises:

1. **Body scan meditation:** Sit or lie down in a comfortable position, close your eyes, and bring your attention to your body. Start at the top of your head and slowly scan down to your toes, paying attention to each part of your body and any sensations you may feel. Take deep breaths and let go of any tension or stress.
2. **Gratitude journaling:** Take a few minutes each day to write down things you are grateful for. This can help shift your focus to the positive and improve your overall mood.
3. **Mindful breathing:** Take a few deep breaths and focus your attention on your breath. Count to four as you inhale, hold for four, and exhale for four. Repeat for several cycles.

Prompts:

1. What are some self-care practices that work well for you?
2. How can you incorporate more physical activity into your daily routine?
3. What are some healthy foods you enjoy eating that you can include in your meals?

Activities:

1. Go for a walk or run outside and take in your surroundings mindfully, paying attention to the sights, sounds, and smells.
2. Take a yoga or meditation class to help reduce stress and improve mindfulness.
3. Cook a healthy meal using fresh, whole ingredients and enjoy it mindfully, savouring each bite.

Mindful reflection: Strategies for reflecting on your progress, learning from your mistakes, and setting new intentions for the future.

Mindful reflection is a crucial aspect of personal and professional growth. It allows you to step back and examine your progress, identify areas for improvement, and set new goals and intentions. Here are some strategies, exercises, prompts, and activities that can help you incorporate mindful reflection into your routine:

1. **Daily journaling:** Set aside a few minutes each day to reflect on your accomplishments, challenges, and emotions. Write down your thoughts and feelings without judgment. This practice can help you develop self-awareness and identify patterns in your behaviour.
2. **Weekly check-ins:** Schedule a weekly meeting with yourself to review your progress towards your goals. Ask yourself what went well, what didn't, and what you can do differently next week. Use this time to celebrate your accomplishments and plan your next steps.
3. **Monthly reflections:** At the end of each month, take a deeper dive into your progress. Review your accomplishments, challenges, and areas for improvement. Ask yourself what you learned, what you need to let go of, and what you want to focus on in the coming month.
4. **Mindful meditation:** Use meditation as a tool for reflection. Set an intention before your meditation practice to reflect on a particular question or issue. After your meditation, write down any insights or realizations that came to you.
5. **Group reflections:** Engage in reflective discussions with colleagues, friends, or family members. Share your experiences, challenges, and successes with one another. Listen deeply and offer support and encouragement.

Some exercises, prompts, and activities for mindful reflection:

1. **Daily journaling:** Set aside 10-15 minutes each day to reflect on your progress, challenges, and successes. Write down your thoughts and feelings, as well as any insights or lessons learned. Consider using prompts such as:

- What was my biggest accomplishment today?
- What did I struggle with today?
- What am I grateful for today?

2. **Weekly check-ins**: At the end of each week, set aside 30 minutes to reflect on your progress over the past week. Consider using prompts such as:

- What were my biggest wins this week?
- What were my biggest challenges this week?
- What did I learn this week?

3. **Monthly goal setting:** At the beginning of each month, set aside time to reflect on your goals and intentions for the month ahead. Consider using prompts such as:

- What are my top priorities for this month?
- What habits do I want to cultivate this month?
- What new skills do I want to learn this month?

4. **Mindful walking:** Take a mindful walk-in nature and use the time to reflect on your progress and intentions. Notice the sights, sounds, and sensations around you and use them as a reminder to stay present and focused. Consider using prompts such as:

- What am I grateful for at this moment?

- What can I let go of that is no longer serving me?
- What small step can I take today to move closer to my goals?

5. **Guided meditations:** Use guided meditations to help you reflect on your progress and set new intentions. Look for meditations that focus on self-reflection, gratitude, and goal setting.

Remember that mindful reflection is a practice, and it may take time to develop a regular habit. Be patient and kind with yourself, and remember that every moment is an opportunity for growth and learning.

CASE STUDIES OF SUCCESSFUL ORGANIZATIONS AND INDIVIDUALS WHO USE MINDFUL PRODUCTIVITY PRACTICES.

Successful organizations that use mindful productivity practices

GOOGLE

Google has a well-established culture of mindfulness and encourages its employees to practice mindfulness in their work and personal lives. The company has implemented a variety of mindfulness programs and practices, including:

1. **Mindful meetings:** Google encourages employees to start meetings with a brief mindfulness practice, such as a short meditation or breathing exercise, to help attendees focus and be present.
2. **Mindful leadership training:** Google offers a Mindful Leadership Program that teaches managers and leaders how to integrate mindfulness into their leadership style and create a more compassionate and supportive work environment.
3. **Mindful cafes:** Google has created mindfulness-themed cafes on its campuses that provide healthy food options and a quiet, peaceful environment for employees to take a break and recharge.
4. **Mindful employee resource groups:** Google has several employee resource groups dedicated to mindfulness and well-being, including the Mindful Awareness Network and the Well-being@Google group.
5. **Mindful meditation rooms:** Google has designated meditation rooms on its campuses where employees can take

a break and meditate or practice mindfulness.

Google has integrated mindful productivity practices into its corporate culture and recognizes the importance of mindfulness for employee well-being and productivity.

APPLE

Apple is a technology company that has incorporated mindful productivity practices into its operations. The company encourages its employees to take breaks and manage their time effectively to improve their productivity and overall well-being.

One way that Apple has incorporated mindfulness practices is through its mindfulness program. The program includes meditation sessions, mindful eating, and stress reduction techniques. The program is designed to help employees reduce stress, improve focus and concentration, and enhance their overall sense of well-being.

Apple has also incorporated mindfulness practices into their work environment. The company has created spaces where employees can relax and recharge, such as quiet rooms, meditation rooms, and outdoor spaces. These spaces are designed to help employees take breaks and refocus, which can improve their productivity and creativity.

Additionally, Apple has implemented strategies to help employees manage their time more effectively. For example, the company encourages employees to use the Pomodoro technique, which involves working for 25 minutes and taking a five-minute break. This technique can help employees stay focused and productive while also taking regular breaks to avoid burnout.

Apple's approach to mindful productivity has been successful, as the company is known for its innovative products and high employee satisfaction ratings. By prioritizing employee well-being and productivity, Apple has created a culture of mindfulness that has benefited both the company and its employees.

INTEL

Intel is a technology company that designs and manufactures semiconductors, processors, and other computer components. The company has incorporated mindful productivity practices into its corporate culture in several ways.

1. **Mindful Leadership:** Intel's CEO, Bob Swan, practices mindful leadership and encourages his leadership team to do the same. They focus on being present and fully engaged in meetings and conversations and actively listening to their team members. This approach helps to foster a culture of trust, respect, and collaboration.
2. **Mindful Communication:** Intel has implemented programs to improve communication and collaboration among team members. The company has established regular check-ins and feedback sessions to ensure that everyone is on the same page and that issues are addressed promptly. They also use communication tools to facilitate teamwork and ensure that everyone has access to the information they need.
3. **Mindful Workspaces:** Intel has created workspaces that promote productivity and well-being. The company has established quiet zones for employees who need to focus on their work and relaxation rooms where employees can take a break and recharge. They also offer wellness programs such as yoga and mindfulness meditation to help employees manage stress and maintain a healthy work-life balance.
4. **Mindful Time Management:** Intel has implemented strategies to help employees manage their time effectively. The company has established clear priorities and deadlines

for projects, and employees are encouraged to use tools and techniques to stay on track. This approach helps to minimize distractions and ensure that work is completed efficiently.

Intel's incorporation of mindful productivity practices has helped the company create a culture that values collaboration, communication, and well-being. This approach has led to increased productivity, higher employee engagement, and improved job satisfaction.

NIKE

Nike, one of the world's leading sportswear and athletic footwear companies, has incorporated various mindful productivity practices to enhance its organizational productivity and employee well-being. Here are some examples of how Nike has incorporated mindful productivity practices:

1. **Mindful Leadership:** Nike has incorporated mindful leadership practices into its management culture, which emphasizes the importance of being present and fully engaged at the moment, listening actively, and showing empathy towards others. The company's leaders are encouraged to lead with compassion and care for their employees, creating a culture of trust and respect.
2. **Mindful Time Management:** Nike has implemented various strategies to help employees manage their time effectively and minimize distractions. The company encourages employees to take regular breaks, prioritize tasks, and delegate responsibilities where necessary. Nike has also implemented tools and software to help employees manage their time more efficiently.
3. **Mindful Communication:** Nike has incorporated mindful communication practices into its organizational culture,

including active listening, effective feedback, and open and honest communication. The company encourages employees to communicate openly and honestly with their colleagues and managers, creating a culture of trust and transparency.

4. **Mindful Self-Care:** Nike recognizes the importance of taking care of employees' physical, mental, and emotional well-being. The company provides various resources and programs to help employees stay healthy and active, including on-site fitness facilities, mindfulness meditation sessions, and wellness programs.
5. **Mindful Innovation:** Nike's innovation team incorporates mindful productivity practices into their ideation and development process. The team emphasizes the importance of being fully present and engaged in the creative process, encouraging employees to take breaks, step away from their work, and recharge their creativity.

Nike has incorporated mindful productivity practices to enhance its organizational culture, employee well-being, and productivity. The company recognizes the importance of being present and engaged at the moment, taking care of employees' physical and emotional well-being, and fostering a culture of trust and transparency.

TARGET

Target, one of the largest retail corporations in the United States, has incorporated mindful productivity practices in various ways to improve its employees' overall well-being and productivity.

One of the ways Target has implemented mindful productivity practices is through the implementation of the "MyDay" program, which is a scheduling tool designed to help employees manage their time effectively. The program helps employees to prioritize tasks, schedule breaks, and avoid burnout. The program is designed to reduce stress levels, increase productivity, and improve overall work-life balance.

Target has also implemented a mindfulness program called "Inner Work Life," which includes training sessions on mindful breathing, body scan meditation, and other mindfulness practices. The program is aimed at reducing stress and increasing employee focus, creativity, and collaboration. The program has been integrated into employee wellness programs, and Target has reported increased engagement and overall satisfaction levels among its employees.

Another way Target has incorporated mindful productivity practices is through the implementation of flexible work arrangements, such as work-from-home policies, compressed workweeks, and job sharing. These arrangements have helped employees to balance their work and personal lives, reduce stress levels, and increase productivity.

Target has also made efforts to create a supportive and inclusive work environment through various initiatives, such as employee resource groups, diversity and inclusion training, and mentorship programs. These initiatives have helped to create a sense of belonging and foster collaboration and innovation among employees.

Target has incorporated mindful productivity practices in various ways, including the implementation of scheduling tools, mindfulness programs, flexible work arrangements, and efforts to create a supportive and inclusive work environment. These practices have helped to improve employee well-being and productivity, leading to better business outcomes.

Successful individuals who use mindful productivity practices

BILL GATES

Bill Gates, the co-founder of Microsoft and one of the richest people in the world, is known for his exceptional productivity and time-management skills. He has been using mindful productivity practices for several years to manage his hectic schedule and achieve his goals.

One of Gates' most well-known mindful productivity practices is his "Think Week," which he has been doing since the early days of Microsoft. During this week, Gates isolates himself in a secluded location with a stack of books and research papers to read and reflect on. He disconnects from all distractions, including technology and even his family, to focus solely on learning and deep thinking.

Gates also incorporates mindfulness practices into his daily routine. He meditates for at least 10 minutes each day, often using guided meditation apps to help him relax and clear his mind. He also practices yoga and other physical activities to maintain his overall well-being.

In addition, Gates is known for his strict time-management practices. He divides his day into five-minute increments and schedules his time meticulously to ensure that he is maximizing his productivity. He also prioritizes his tasks by importance and delegates lower-priority tasks to his assistants or team members to free up more time for strategic work.

Bill Gates' use of mindful productivity practices has helped him achieve incredible success in his career while also maintaining his well-being and a healthy work-life balance.

RICHARD BRANSON

Richard Branson, the founder of Virgin Group, is a well-known advocate of mindfulness and meditation as tools for productivity and success. Branson has spoken about his personal meditation practice and how it helps him to stay focused and calm amidst the chaos of running a large and diverse company.

In addition to his personal practice, Branson has also incorporated mindfulness and meditation into the culture of Virgin Group. The company offers mindfulness and meditation training to employees and encourages them to take breaks throughout the day to meditate or simply clear their minds.

Branson has also emphasized the importance of work-life balance and believes that taking time to rest and recharge is essential for productivity and creativity. He has spoken about his own habits of taking breaks to exercise or spend time with his family and encourages his employees to prioritize self-care as well.

Richard Branson's approach to mindful productivity emphasizes the importance of taking care of oneself and finding ways to stay focused and calm amidst the pressures of running a business.

TIM FERRISS

Tim Ferriss is a well-known entrepreneur, author, and podcaster who has incorporated various mindful productivity practices into his daily routine. Some examples include:

1. **Setting priorities:** Ferriss starts each day by identifying the most important task that he needs to accomplish. This helps him to stay focused and avoid getting bogged down by less important tasks.
2. **Time-blocking:** Ferriss is a big believer in time-blocking, which involves scheduling specific times for certain activities. This helps him to stay on track and avoid wasting time on unimportant tasks.
3. **Meditation:** Ferriss practices mindfulness meditation for at least 20 minutes every morning. This helps him to clear his mind and improve his focus throughout the day.
4. **Exercise:** Ferriss is also a big proponent of regular exercise, which he says helps him to stay energized and focused.

5. **Regular breaks:** Ferriss takes regular breaks throughout the day to avoid burnout and maintain his productivity. For example, he might take a short walk or meditate for a few minutes between tasks.

Tim Ferriss's approach to mindful productivity emphasizes the importance of setting priorities, managing time effectively, and taking care of both physical and mental well-being.

OPRAH WINFREY

Oprah Winfrey is known for her successful career as a television personality, producer, and philanthropist. She is also known for her dedication to self-improvement and mindfulness practices.

One of the ways Oprah Winfrey uses mindful productivity practices is by starting her day with meditation and journaling. She has spoken publicly about how she takes time each morning to meditate and reflect on her goals and intentions for the day. She also writes down affirmations and positive thoughts in her journal, which helps her stay focused and motivated throughout the day.

Another way Oprah uses mindful productivity practices is by setting boundaries and prioritizing self-care. She talked about how important it is to take care of yourself first before taking care of others or tackling work tasks. She makes sure to get enough sleep, exercise regularly, and eat healthy foods. She also takes breaks throughout the day to rest and recharge, which helps her maintain her energy and focus.

In addition, Oprah practices mindful communication by actively listening to others and expressing empathy and compassion. She has talked about the importance of being present and fully engaged in conversations and taking the time to understand others' perspectives.

Oprah Winfrey's use of mindful productivity practices has helped her achieve great success in her career and personal life while also prioritizing her well-being and relationships with others.

ARIANNA HUFFINGTON

Arianna Huffington, the co-founder of The Huffington Post, is known for promoting the importance of self-care and mindful productivity practices. She has emphasized the need for individuals to prioritize their well-being in order to achieve success in both their personal and professional lives.

One of the ways Huffington incorporates mindfulness into her daily routine is by practising meditation. She has said that meditation helps her to focus and be more productive, and she even has a meditation room in her office. She also promotes the benefits of getting enough sleep and unplugging from technology and has written a book on the topic, "The Sleep Revolution: Transforming Your Life, One Night at a Time."

In addition, Huffington emphasizes the importance of setting boundaries and saying "no" when necessary in order to avoid burnout and overwhelm. She has said that saying "no" to things that are not aligned with our values or goals can actually be empowering and lead to greater productivity and fulfilment in the long run.

Huffington also promotes the idea of "micro-steps", or small, manageable actions that can be taken toward achieving larger goals. By breaking down big tasks into smaller, more manageable steps, individuals can avoid feeling overwhelmed and build momentum toward achieving their goals.

Arianna Huffington's approach to mindful productivity emphasizes the importance of taking care of oneself in order to achieve success and incorporates practices such as meditation, setting boundaries, and breaking down goals into smaller steps.

PERSONAL ANECDOTES AND STORIES FROM THE AUTHOR AND OTHERS WHO HAVE TRANSFORMED THEIR WORK AND LIVES WITH MINDFULNESS.

The Author's personal journey has transformed his work and life with mindfulness.

As the author of this book, I have had my own personal journey with mindfulness and how it has transformed my work and life. At first, I was sceptical of the idea of mindfulness and meditation. I thought it was something that only spiritual or religious people did, and I didn't see how it could benefit my busy and hectic life.

But as I delved deeper into the research and spoke to people who had incorporated mindfulness into their lives, I began to realize the incredible potential it had to transform not only my work but also my overall well-being. I started small, with just a few minutes of meditation each day, and gradually worked my way up to longer sessions.

At first, I struggled with incorporating mindfulness into my routine. I found it difficult to quiet my mind and focus on my breath, and I often felt restless and distracted. But with practice and patience, I began to notice the benefits of mindfulness in my work and life.

I found that I was more focused and productive at work, and I was able to approach my tasks with a sense of calm and clarity that I had never experienced before. I also noticed that I was more present in my personal life, able to enjoy the small moments and connect more deeply with the people around me.

My personal journey with mindfulness has been transformative, and I am excited to share the tools and techniques that have helped me with others who are looking to incorporate mindfulness into their own lives.

MARC BENIOFF, THE FOUNDER AND CEO OF SALESFORCE'S STORY

A successful entrepreneur who has incorporated mindfulness practices into their work is Marc Benioff, the founder, and CEO of Salesforce, a cloud-based software company. Benioff has been a vocal advocate for mindfulness and has credited it with helping him become a more effective leader.

Benioff first discovered mindfulness when he was dealing with stress and burnout while running Salesforce. He started practising meditation and yoga and soon found that it helped him manage his stress levels and stay focused on his goals.

Over time, Benioff began to incorporate mindfulness into his leadership style. He created a mindfulness room at Salesforce's headquarters, where employees can go to meditate and recharge. He also encourages his employees to take breaks throughout the day to recharge and refresh their minds.

Benioff has also made mindfulness a core part of Salesforce's corporate culture. The company offers mindfulness training to its employees and has integrated mindfulness practices into its management and leadership training programs.

As a result of these efforts, Salesforce has been recognized as one of the most innovative and successful companies in the world. Benioff has been named one of the most influential business leaders in the world, and Salesforce has consistently been ranked as one of the best places to work.

Overall, Benioff's story shows how incorporating mindfulness practices into your work can help you manage stress, stay focused, and become a more effective leader. By making mindfulness a core part of your corporate culture, you can create a more productive and successful workplace.

THE STORY OF JEFF WEINER, THE FORMER CEO OF LINKEDIN

A noteworthy entrepreneur who has incorporated mindfulness practices into his work is Jeff Weiner, the former CEO of LinkedIn. In an interview with Oprah Winfrey, Weiner shared how he began practising mindfulness to combat his own feelings of stress and anxiety.

Weiner described how he felt overwhelmed with the constant demands of his job and the pressure to constantly be available and responsive. He realized that he needed to find a way to manage his stress and cultivate a sense of calm in order to be more productive and effective in his work.

Weiner began practising meditation and mindfulness, which helped him develop greater self-awareness and emotional intelligence. He started to notice when he was becoming stressed or reactive and was able to pause and respond in a more thoughtful and intentional way.

Through his mindfulness practice, Weiner also developed a greater sense of empathy for his colleagues and employees. He recognized that everyone was dealing with their own stress and challenges and began to approach his interactions with more compassion and understanding.

Weiner's mindfulness practice has had a profound impact on his leadership style and the culture of his company. Under his leadership, LinkedIn became known for its focus on employee well-being, including offering on-site meditation and mindfulness programs.

Weiner credits his mindfulness practice for helping him lead with greater clarity, compassion, and purpose and for creating a culture that values both productivity and well-being.

ACTRESS EMMA WATSON'S STORY

One successful star who has spoken openly about experiencing burnout and turning to mindfulness is actress Emma Watson. In a 2019 interview with British Vogue, she discussed how she had taken a year off from acting to focus on her personal development and self-care.

During this time, Watson practised daily meditation and also attended a week-long silent retreat. She described the experience as life-changing, saying it gave her a new perspective on her own thoughts and emotions. She also began prioritizing her physical health, focusing on regular exercise and a healthy diet.

As a result of her mindfulness practices and self-care, Watson was able to return to acting with renewed energy and focus. She explained in the interview, "I feel very differently about my work now. I'm more confident and passionate about it than I've ever been."

Watson's experience shows the power of mindfulness and self-care in recovering from burnout and finding renewed purpose and energy in one's career.

THE STORY OF CHRISSY TEIGEN, MODEL, AUTHOR, AND TELEVISION PERSONALITY

Chrissy Teigen, a model, author, and television personality, has spoken publicly about her struggles with anxiety and how mindfulness has helped her find greater balance in her life. In an interview with People Magazine, Teigen described how she turned to meditation and mindfulness practices to help manage her anxiety and prioritize her mental health.

Teigen shared that she struggled with constantly trying to please others and be available to everyone at all times, which left her feeling overwhelmed and burnt out. She found that practising mindfulness helped her become more present at the moment and better able to prioritize her own needs.

Teigen started with simple mindfulness practices, such as taking a few deep breaths before responding to stressful situations and practising gratitude for the good things in her life. She also began meditating regularly, even if it was just for a few minutes a day.

Through these practices, Teigen found that she was better able to balance her work and personal life, saying, "I'm learning that it's okay to say no, it's okay to take time for yourself, and it's okay to prioritize your own mental health."

Teigen's story is a reminder that even celebrities can struggle with work-life balance and mental health and that mindfulness practices can be a helpful tool in finding greater balance and peace in life.

KATY PERRY, SUPERSTAR POP SINGER'S STORY

Another personality who has spoken about her struggles with productivity and how mindfulness helped them is Katy Perry. In an interview with Glamour magazine, she talked about how she used to be a workaholic and would push herself to the point of exhaustion. She realized that she needed to make a change when she found herself crying in her car on the way to a meeting.

Katy started practising mindfulness through meditation and prayer, which helped her become more centred and focused. She learned to prioritize her self-care and take breaks when she needed them. As a result, she found that she was able to work more efficiently and effectively without burning out.

In an interview with Forbes, Katy said, "I meditate, and I pray every day. I think that has given me a lot of grounding and a lot of peace, and it's really helped me with my mental health. And I think that's why I'm able to have a healthy career and healthy relationships. Because I put that before anything else."

CHAPTER 10

CONCLUSION: EMBRACING A MINDFUL PRODUCTIVITY LIFESTYLE

SUMMARY OF KEY TAKEAWAYS FROM THE BOOK

In this book, we explored the concept of mindful productivity and how it can help individuals achieve more by doing less. Throughout the chapters, we discussed various strategies and techniques for incorporating mindfulness into our daily lives, both at work and at home.

As we come to the conclusion of this book, let's review some of the key takeaways that can help us embrace a mindful productivity lifestyle:

1. **Understanding the benefits of mindfulness:** Mindfulness can help us reduce stress, increase focus, and improve overall well-being. By taking a few moments each day to practice mindfulness, we can become more productive and efficient in our work.
2. **Setting clear intentions and goals: By** setting clear intentions and goals, we can focus our energy and attention on what is most important to us. Mindful goal setting can help us prioritize our tasks and achieve our desired outcomes.
3. **Practising self-awareness:** Mindful productivity begins with self-awareness. By being aware of our thoughts, emotions,

and behaviours, we can make conscious choices about how we spend our time and energy.

4. **Cultivating a growth mindset:** A growth mindset allows us to view challenges as opportunities for growth and learning. By embracing this mindset, we can approach our work with a sense of curiosity and openness.
5. **Creating healthy habits:** Mindful productivity is not just about what we do but also how we do it. By creating healthy habits around our sleep, diet, exercise, and work environment, we can support our overall well-being and productivity.

By embracing these key takeaways and incorporating mindful productivity practices into our daily lives, we can achieve more by doing less and living a more fulfilling and balanced life.

HOW TO CONTINUE APPLYING MINDFUL PRODUCTIVITY PRINCIPLES IN YOUR DAILY LIFE

Incorporating mindful productivity principles into your daily life can be challenging, but it is essential for achieving sustainable success and well-being. Here are some practical tips for continuing to apply the principles of mindful productivity in your daily life:

1. **Start Small:** It's important to remember that incorporating mindful productivity principles into your daily routine is a process. Start with small changes, such as taking breaks during work hours or setting aside time for self-care activities like meditation or exercise. Over time, you can gradually build on these changes and incorporate more mindful practices into your daily routine.
2. **Stay Consistent:** Consistency is key when it comes to incorporating mindful productivity principles into your daily routine. Try to establish a routine that works for you and stick to it as best you can. This will help you develop good habits and make mindful productivity a part of your daily life.
3. **Reflect and Evaluate:** It's important to regularly reflect on your progress and evaluate what is working and what isn't. This will help you identify areas where you can improve and adjust your routine accordingly.
4. **Find an Accountability Partner:** Having someone to hold you accountable can be a great way to stay on track with your mindful productivity goals. Consider finding a friend or colleague who is also interested in practising mindful productivity and checking in with each other regularly to share progress and provide support.

5. **Keep Learning:** Mindful productivity is an ongoing journey, and there is always more to learn. Keep seeking out new resources, books, and courses to deepen your understanding and practice mindful productivity.

By incorporating these tips into your daily routine, you can continue to apply the principles of mindful productivity and achieve greater success and well-being in your life.

ENCOURAGEMENT AND INSPIRATION FOR READERS TO CREATE A MORE FULFILLING AND SUSTAINABLE WORK AND LIFE BALANCE.

In the final chapter of this book, I would like to encourage and inspire readers to create a more fulfilling and sustainable work and life balance.

I understand that incorporating mindful productivity practices into your daily life can be a challenging process, but it is essential for your overall well-being and success. Therefore, I want to offer some encouragement and inspiration to help you on this journey.

Firstly, it is essential to remember that creating a mindful, productive lifestyle is not about perfection. It's about progress. Every small step towards incorporating mindfulness practices into your daily routine is a step in the right direction. Be kind to yourself and celebrate the small victories along the way.

Secondly, make sure to focus on what's most important to you. We all have different priorities and goals, and it's crucial to identify what those are and align your daily actions with them. This way, you can avoid getting caught up in busy work and focus on what truly matters to you.

Thirdly, find a support system. Incorporating mindful productivity practices can be challenging, but having a supportive community can make all the difference. Whether it's friends, family, or a mentor, having someone to hold you accountable and offer encouragement can be incredibly valuable.

Lastly, remember that creating a mindful, productive lifestyle is a journey, not a destination. There will be ups and downs along the way, but if you stay committed and consistent, you will see the benefits in your work and personal life. I sincerely hope that this book has provided you with valuable insights and tools to help you on your journey toward a more fulfilling and sustainable work and life balance.